AR &
BEVERAGE
OPERATION

Ensuring Success & Maximum Profit

By Chris Parry

The Food Service Professional's Guide To:
Bar & Beverage Operation Ensuring Success &
Maximum Profit: 365 Secrets Revealed

Atlantic Publishing Group, Inc. Copyright © 2003
1210 SW 23rd Place
Ocala, Florida 34474
800-541-1336
352-622-5836 - Fax

www.atlantic-pub.com - Web Site
sales@atlantic-pub.com E-mail

SAN Number :268-1250

International Standard Book Number: 0-910627-21-5

Library of Congress Cataloging-in-Publication Data

Parry, Chris, 1956-
Ensuring your bar & beverage operation is a success : 365
secrets revealed / by Chris Parry, Douglas Robert Brown.
p. cm. -- (The food service professionals guide to ; 11)
Includes bibliographical references and index.
ISBN 0-910627-21-5 (pbk. : alk. paper)
1. Bartending. 2. Food service management. I. Brown,
Douglas Robert, 1960- . II. Title. III. Title: Ensuring your
bar and beverage operation is a success. IV. Series.
TX950.7.P37 2003
647.95'068--dc21
2002010830

Printed in Canada

Book layout and design by Meg Buchner of Megadesign
www.mega-designs.com • e-mail: megadesn@mhtc.net

CONTENTS

325988

New ideas to make your bar and beverage operation a success.

INTRODUCTION

Running a bar is perceived by many outside the hospitality industry to be a relatively simple vocation. But to those whose job it is to make sure that their customers have an outstanding outing, the employees don't disappear with the take, and the owners maintain a steadily rising profit margin, the daily grind of running a bar is nothing compared to the tension that comes from trying to figure out how to take it to the next level.

That's where our book comes in. If we can help you relax, concentrate on your core business and learn just one new idea every day that you can easily implement within your establishment, then this publication will have paid for itself a thousand times over by year's end — and your bar operation will be on the fast track to "next big thing" status. Perhaps some of these tips won't apply to you, but one thing is for sure: plenty of them will.

Enjoy!

Running a bar and beverage operation isn't only about slinging beers.

CHAPTER ONE

THE BASICS

Fill a Local Need

Running a bar and beverage operation isn't only about slinging beers and mopping up afterwards. In fact, there are a lot of basic business techniques that apply as much to the hospitality industry as they do to any other. If you don't know these simple business techniques, it can really cost you! Okay then, what's the first step on the way to success? A national ad campaign? A celebrity-riddled black-tie party? Perhaps down the track, but for now let's start off with a little solid planning. Follow these simple steps and by the end, you'll have the road map to success:

- **Take a look at the competition.** Before you even make your first alteration to your business, spend an hour sitting in each competing establishment in your area. Take notes. Who frequents these bars? Older patrons? Younger patrons? Yuppies? Tradespeople? What sort of bar is it? What do they charge? How busy are they and on which night are they busiest? What are they doing wrong? What are they doing right?

- **Lower prices.** If competitors' prices are high, you might consider lowering yours. Not always the cure-all, but lower prices are certainly worth considering, if only to get people to try your establishment for the first time.

- **Service.** If your competitors' standards of service are low, you might put added emphasis on your own. Encourage your employees to make your customers feel wanted. It's a no-lose situation. Label yourself "the friendliest bar in town."

- **Opening hours.** If the competition stops their food service early, consider keeping yours open late. Quite often a hungry patron will leave a bar in search of late-night food, and if he or she finds the way to you, you might have just snatched a new regular.

- **Special promotions.** If your competitors are filled to the gills on Thursday nights, it might be prudent to put your energies into special promotions on Wednesdays, or Fridays. Avoid using your best ideas and resources trying to compete on someone else's strongest night.

Define Your Customer Base

When you've done a little market research on your competition and addressed your strengths and their weaknesses, you'll need to decide on your target market. Sure, "everyone" buys Coca-Cola, but that company doesn't waste time and money marketing their product to "every" demographic. Instead they focus their attack on one particular area of the market (16-to 35-year-olds) and focus their resources targeting that one group, knowing full well that if they can win them over, the others will follow.

- **Tempt local workers.** Are there a large number of blue-collar industries close to your location? If so, appeal to their tastes. Rather than setting up a wine bar, consider a sports bar. Offer incentives for local workers to make your place their afternoon stopover.

- **Live music.** It doesn't necessarily cost a lot to feature live music, and the bands you feature don't always have to be loud either. Quite often an acoustic performance can outdraw a heavy rock concert. It can also enhance the atmosphere of your establishment in the process.

- **Consider the young crowd.** Is there a college, which could be a good supply of younger patrons, within a few miles? If you ran a few specials, you could certainly draw in a younger crowd.

- **Attract tourists.** Is there a large hotel nearby? If so, you could attract tourists by advertising in local tourist guides. Look beyond your traditional walk-by traffic. Consider working by nontraditional means to draw in people from surrounding areas.

- **Dare to be different.** Are all the other local bars loud or "low rent"? Is there a need for somewhere quiet and comfortable where people can sip a coffee instead of a beer and enjoy a quiet meal? Fill this need.

Expand Your Customer Base

So you've managed to bring together a core of regular patrons, but how do you go beyond the constrictions of that slice of the market and bring in a wider variety of customers without driving away your existing business? Consider the following:

- **Take it slowly.** Transform your customer base slowly. It's the surest way to bring in a new segment of the market. Lure new customers over the long-term while making sure that your existing clientele are never made uncomfortable. If you change things too quickly, your core regulars may begin to feel that their favorite haunt is no longer "theirs."

- **Jazz night.** An older crowd might enjoy some live jazz music, which in turn will bring in a younger audience that appreciates the music and atmosphere as somewhere to "warm up" before they move on to somewhere louder afterwards.

- **Stand-up comedy.** Give the young male crowd a reason to bring their friends, girlfriends, wives and workmates along. Introduce a stand-up comedy night. It may bring in a whole group of people who might otherwise never have set foot in your bar.

- **Choose entertainers carefully.** The kind of crowd that would come to see a live punk band might be a rude shock to your over-45-year-old regulars, but your regulars are far less likely to take issue with a country and western band, a 70s cover band or a solo act.

- **Attract female clientele.** A beer-guzzling sports bar crowd is never going to get into a wine-tasting night, but they may well appreciate it when the ladies begin to arrive and the gender ratio starts to even out!

Engage in Continuous Market Research

The term "market research" sends many mom-and-pop bar operators into glazed-over-eye mode, but the simple fact of the matter is that knowing what your customers think about your establishment is vital. Ignore popular opinion at your peril.

- **Do more than asking the regulars** what they think of your establishment. Talk to non-customers. Find out what it would take to bring them into your establishment. Lower prices? Live entertainment? Dancing? Can they see what you have to offer as they walk by? Do they know how good your food is?

- **Try talking to your competitions' customers.** Find out where the other bars have you beat. Talk to them often so that when the landscape changes, you know about it.

- **Keep asking questions about the neighborhood.** For example, a geographical area can change markedly with a labor shift at a large local company or the redirection of a roadway, or even an alteration to a bus route.

- **The competition is constantly shifting.** A competitor can suddenly become a major player with one successful promotion, price adjustment or addition to their list of products and services. Keep your finger on the pulse. Don't miss a golden opportunity.

- **Your market is shifting, too.** Take a look at the ratio of sales between your different types of alcohol (draft beer, bottled beer, spirits, liqueurs, wine). Do you think your market is shifting? Has there been a recent increase in draft beer and spirits sales? Perhaps the blue-collar boys are moving in.... Think about adding a few bar snacks to your menu.

- **Act on what your market research tells you.** If something needs changing, change it. If something just needs a small tweak, tweak it. Micromanage everything - the little things really do count.

Sample Market Research Questions

Here are some simple questions to ask your customers that can help streamline your business. For results, try the following:

- Do you sometimes visit a competitor's establishment? If so, why?

- What nights are the other places you visit slow? Which nights are they busy?

- Is the outside of the premises inviting to a casual passer-by?

- What would you like to see changed about your establishment?

- Which staff members are your favorites? Why?

- Do you like our food? Do you have any suggestions for new items?

- How did you first find us, and what brings you back?

- Would higher prices drive you away?

- Would lower prices get you in more often?

- Do you bring friends to our bar? If no, why not?

- Do our hours of operation suit your needs?

Would Your Bar Benefit from a New Theme?

A few decades ago, the casinos of Las Vegas figured out that the gambling dollar would only stretch so far, but the entertainment and family travel dollar could bring in practically unlimited new sources of revenue. As a result, the powers that be built humongous theme casinos, such as Caesar's Palace, The Paris, and The New York. Big scale, sure! But would a smaller-scale theme benefit your establishment?

- **Margarita night.** Talk to your tequila distributor about how they can help you hold a margarita night - either with giveaways or décor or a deal on tequila that will allow you to lower prices for a night every week.

- **Cater for the sports-minded.** A little sports memorabilia, a pool table and a big-screen TV can turn a nondescript back room into a sports fan's dream. With a few coin-operated games thrown in, it could be a nice little earner. Sports memorabilia can be bought quickly and inexpensively through online auction Web sites, such as eBay (www.ebay.com).

- **Quiet room**. If there's a college close to your establishment, a quiet room in the back could easily be outfitted to be a "study bar." Simply provide comfortable seating, larger tables, power outlets for laptops, soft lights and a quiet atmosphere. Market the area to students as a good place to sit and study and, of course, enjoy a drink.

- **Irish pub theme.** Brewing companies like Guinness have a vested interest in promoting the "Irish pub" theme, as people who go to an Irish pub are more likely to try an Irish beer. As a result, these companies have people on staff whose job it is to help turn your bar into an authentic Irish pub. Talk to your local rep and see what they can do to help.

- **Create ambiance.** Some wood paneling, a little mood lighting, maybe a giant fish tank behind the bar, and some exotic drinks on the menu might instantly transform your bland four-walled room into an island bar. Or, consider a 1960s-style schlock tiki lounge that the "alternative" crowd will eat up.

- **Themes.** In short, a plain "drinking bar" can do good business by itself. But with a well-executed theme backing it up, especially if said theme doesn't make the casual drinker uncomfortable, your bar can add to its existing business and multiply that existing business in the process.

Observe the Successful

You don't have to look far to find a successful "theme" establishment in the hospitality industry. Every Main Street has a fine selection of operations that have used a theme to enhance their existing business. For example:

- **The Caribbean theme.** The Bahama Breeze bar/restaurant chain follows a Caribbean flavor and entertains customers with steel drum music while feeding them "jerk chicken pizzas" and slinging garnish-heavy island cocktails. Island décor, bright staff uniforms, a few palm trees, a unique menu - customers feel like tourists without flying to the tropics!

- **Sing along.** For example, the Bar at Times Square in the New York-New York Hotel and Casino in Las Vegas is a little corner bar featuring two dueling piano players who boast that they know the lyrics to just about any song you can name. The place is packed to "standing room only" every night of the week as locals and tourists cram in, drink a ton and sing along.

- **Rock music memorabilia.** The Hard Rock Café has based a global bar/restaurant empire on memorabilia, rock music and good burgers. It's as much a museum chain as it is a bar chain. But it's a winning formula.

- **Blues and jazz.** The House of Blues started out as a place to see jazz and blues music, but they're such an innovative company that they now host the biggest concerts (in the smallest rooms) of any bar chain. Their "Louisiana bayou" theme goes down great - and so do the beers.

- **Nostalgia.** The Double Down Saloon in Las Vegas is a small bar that boasts a jukebox featuring the world's most eclectic collection of music, TV screens that show 1940s adventure serials and midget pornography, and a drinks menu featuring concoctions with names like "ass juice." Tacky? Sure, but it's a huge crowd draw in a city that has plenty of draws already.

Try a Theme for a Night

Do you have to totally transform your bar to run with a theme? Not at all - in fact, one-off nights can be a great testing ground to see what might work over the long-term. Consider these for a change from the everyday:

- **Wine-tasting night.** It might bring in a new type of clientele. A regularly scheduled wine-tasting night might totally transform your establishment. Any wine distributor will gladly assist.

- **Cigar night.** In conjunction with a local tobacconist, consider setting up a cigar lounge. The event is likely to bring in a bigger-spending crowd than you're used to.

- **Do you have a stage that isn't being used during the day?** Put an ad in the local alternative and college newspapers offering the stage area as a free rehearsal space for local bands (with volume restrictions of course) during the daytime hours. You may well begin to draw a live music crowd in the process. Best of all, this is during your slowest bar hours.

- **Movie night.** Contact a local video store that can supply you with pre-release movies in return for a little cross-promotion. Not only will it bring in new business, but it will also keep your customers seated for hours longer than they might normally have stayed.

- **Karaoke.** It's often worth the outlay of a few hundred dollars to run a karaoke night. These nights are usually very successful at bringing in new and repeat business.

- **Sporting events can be a big crowd-puller.** If you're situated near a sporting stadium or a college campus, you're on to a winner! The after-event crowd can bring in big business. Run a special before or after each game. If you don't have a game nearby, keep an eye on the sporting calendar and show the big events on a big screen.

- **Cater for big spenders.** Jazz bands tend to draw an older and more dedicated audience with plenty of money to spend. An added bonus is that jazz bands don't need a lot of equipment to set up.

- **Real ale.** The microbrewery business is still big business. Even if you don't brew your own beer, turn your bar into a boutique-beer-themed establishment. It'll draw the dedicated from far and wide to sample your impressive array of ales.

- **Country and Western music has a big following.** Even in areas where this type of music isn't considered a big deal, there are usually enough fans of the genre to fill a good C&W bar, especially if it features live music or - dare we say it - line dancing. A western theme, some Tex-Mex cooking, and you're halfway there.

- **Tourist attractions.** A little memorabilia can be a big tourist attraction. Establishments like the Hard Rock Café and Planet Hollywood do a brisk business with their memorabilia collections. You, too, can pull in big numbers if you have a "hook" to get people in the door to look at your walls. Companies such as American Heritage USA can provide you with everything from barber chairs to antique tin signs to old neon clocks. See more at www.americanheritageusa.com, or call 714-289-2241.

- **Geography-specific themes are a simple way to go.** An English pub or a Wild West saloon doesn't necessarily need to be located in London or the desert. Quite often a country or location-specific theme can bring in a deluge of expatriates and tourists from that part of the planet - not to mention give your locals a pleasant escape from the everyday.

Is your bar set up to allow maximum productivity?

CHAPTER TWO

THE HARDWARE

Bar Design

The way your bar operates depends on many factors, one of the most important being the "machinery" of the bar. Sometimes, no matter how efficient your staff, the bar just isn't set up to allow maximum productivity. Avoid that happening to your bar.

- **Form over function?** Think hard about potential consequences before spending too much money on interior design. Of course, how a bar is perceived aesthetically is very important. But, don't put aesthetics above function. It could radically hurt your business. Before starting on the renovations, stop and think about how they will affect your staff and the duties they have to fulfill.

- **Cramped working areas reduce productivity.** Make sure the new bar has enough room for bartenders and glass collectors to move about freely.

- **Storage space.** Is there enough storage space behind your bar to ensure your stock doesn't run dry three times a night? Consider extra fridge space or even bins full of ice for fast-selling bottled beer products.

- **Is the bar décor comfortable, attractive and easy to clean?** Not only does clutter look bad; it can reduce productivity.

- **Comfort.** Are your seats and tables the sort of quality furnishing that will keep a customer happily seated throughout the evening? A little more money spent on customer comfort will translate into dollars over the bar.

The Front Bar

Your front bar is your first line of attack in the fight to keep a customer coming back for more. When looking for ways to impress your clientele, remember that the impression this bar leaves on your patrons is of paramount importance. Consider these issues and make sure the design of your front bar works as well as it can:

- **Customer interaction is vital.** Is your bar top too wide? Is the music too loud for a customer's order to be heard over a crowd? Does it inhibit your staff from being able to engage in friendly chat with your clientele? Interaction with your customers is crucial if you're going to turn one-off customers into regulars.

- **Be wary of mirrors.** Mirrors may give a momentary illusion of more space, but they also fog up and smear an hour after they're cleaned. Mirrors might look good initially, but their maintenance does cost you money. Consider replacing them with artwork, memorabilia, menu boards, or something else that will draw people in. Don't just fill a space.

- **Appearances count.** Do you have bits of paper stuck to the walls which might contain important information for your staff but look terrible to the customers? Make sure that any staff notices are out of your customers' eye line.

- **Design a bottle display with enough space to add to your inventory easily.** A good selection of wines, beers, spirits and liqueurs is an essential part of a popular bar operation. You should always be looking to introduce your customers to something new.

- **Stock requisitions.** Is there enough room on your bottle display to accommodate two bottles of each brand? When one bottle runs out, you don't want your staff to have to dig around a stock room for a replacement. Talk to a bar fitter about improving your bottle display. Add capacity. A small expense now can bring you future benefits.

- **Make it easy for your customers to see what you have on tap.** Can your customers see what draft beers you have without craning their necks? Do patrons have to ask the bartender what's on offer every few minutes? If you watch the bar staff closely, you'll see that they spend a lot of time telling customers what beers you stock. Solve the problem by adding a small draft beer menu to each table and another on the wall behind the bar. Have the menus professionally prepared so that they add to, rather than detract from, your bar's appearance.

- **Is your entire inventory on display?** Are your fridges in plain view? Floor fridges make access difficult for your staff. They also hide your product lines from your customers. Consider changing the setup behind your bar so that most of your fridge space is in clear view.

Good Hygiene through Planning

A good front bar should be truly impressive upon first glimpse. An expansive selection of spirits and liqueurs can be an impressive sight. So, too, can a personable, neat and tidy bartender in a well-pressed uniform, greeting the customers like an old friend. But, the first time a customer finds anything less than clean about a bar, the impression they take home will be a bad one. Thankfully, some smart bar design can go a long way towards helping staff keep your establishment spotlessly clean.

- **Avoid "tight corners."** Some surfaces are a lot easier to keep clean than others. Nothing is surer to collect "bar gunk" than a tight corner. Frankly, your customers have a right to expect a comfortable level of cleanliness. Anything less is likely to draw their wrath, if not the attention of local health inspectors! Make sure your employees keep any tight corners as clean as they keep the flat surfaces. Do regular inspections to make sure.

- **Make it a habit to line all ice sinks with plastic trash bags.** Whenever your staff needs to clean out the sink (either because of a glass breakage or as part of regular bar cleaning) they simply can remove the bag - ice, water and all. It is easy to replace without inhibiting service. This will add a small cost to the maintenance of your bar, but the payoff in terms of cleanliness and service speed will be considerable.

- **Glass-cleaning areas should be scrubbed several times a day.** These areas should always be out of the customers' field of vision. Your customers should never glimpse your bar's engine. Ensure that all boxes, empty glass racks and dirty glasses are kept out of sight, either in "under-bar" sinks or "out-of-view" back-bar areas.

Consider Customer Comfort

Have you ever sat under a blue neon light for an hour? While neon décor might look great when a bar is packed to capacity and the music is pumping, when business is slow it's like a power drill closing in on the center of your forehead. Certainly your customers should be impressed by your décor, but will the very look that draws them in end up driving them away early? Consider the following:

- **Invest in comfortable seating.** Wooden barstools may look fine, and are usually very cheap to purchase and maintain, but are they likely to give your patrons buttock cramps after an hour? Try padded seating. Make sure the customers can move their seats to suit with a minimum of fuss - never have barstools and tables bolted to the floor.

- **Consider installing booths.** Replace those cheap tables. If you want your customers to stay all night, give them the kind of seats that will make them too comfortable to leave. Customers tend to settle into booths, especially if a venue is crowded. If your drink servers are attentive and food is available, a group in a booth is all the more likely to settle in until closing. Remember, a shaky table is very easy to walk away from.

- **A comfortable bar surface keeps your clientele happy.** Make sure your customers can lean on the bar and get comfy without getting cold elbows. This is much more likely if your bar surface is wood than if it's stainless steel or marble.

- **Lighting.** Your lighting does more than just keep people from bumping into one another - it sets a mood. If you've inherited a system of overhead fluorescent lights or neon, consider getting a lighting specialist to give you suggestions on potential improvements. It won't cost as much as you think. Generally a quote is free.

Color Schemes Influence Buyer Behavior

Have you ever wondered why fast-food outlets almost always follow the same color scheme? The McDonald's décor and logo are yellow and red, as are those of Taco Bell and Burger King; KFC's are red and white, just like Pizza Hut, Wendy's and Jack in the Box. Coincidence? Not quite. Research has shown that certain colors promote cravings in consumers. When an establishment is decked out in reds and yellows, customers tend to experience feelings of hunger, not to mention an inability to settle down and relax. It's believed that those colors will cause a moderately hungry person to order a little more than he or she needs. They also will prompt customers to move on quickly once their money is spent. Blues and greens, on the other hand, promote relaxation, serenity and even lethargy amongst customers, which might be the better option for an establishment like a bar, where you're looking to keep your clientele seated for the long haul. How can you utilize these colors to quietly "persuade" your customers to buy, buy and buy?

- **Menus and food areas.** A red and yellow color scheme on your tabletop menus or food area signage may cause your patrons to develop a stronger urge to order food, yet not be so over-whelming as to chase them out the door.

- **Bar décor.** Some hardy potted plants, maybe a few palms and a little pastel color on your walls may help your bar promote a feeling of island-like serenity in your customers, compelling them to relax a little - and stay.

- **External décor.** Your signage and building front are supposed to draw people in. But does your frontage inspire the desire to party? Or does it drive people to the KFC down the street?

- **Staff uniforms.** Do the colors of your employees' uniforms say to your customers, "Welcome, stay a while," or "I'm busy, what do you want?" Your staff uniforms are an important part of your overall décor. Your decisions about their design can radically change the atmosphere of your establishment.

Service Streamlining

When you design your service area, it's important to realize that every step a bartender takes in the serving of a drink is costing you money and making your customers impatient. Where does your staff need to walk to get a clean glass? How far from there to the ice bins and then to the spirit dispenser? And where are your soda guns in relation to the bottles? Is the cash register yet another trip away from the customer? Even if your bartender has to take only four or five steps between each of these posts, consider how far that means your bartender has to walk in the course of serving 500 drinks a night! This is bad enough for a solo bartender, but when two or three people are working behind the same bar and sharing facilities, it can be an unproductive nightmare.

- **Most bartenders are right-handed.** With this in mind, your bar setup should allow your staff to pick up glasses with their left hands and bottles with their right, so that the drink creation process is at its most productive. If your bottles are on the left and glasses on the right, your people will do a lot of crisscrossing back and forth, resulting in more time taken to prepare a drink - and a lot more breakage and spillage.

- **Consider your customers.** If they're lined up three deep to get a drink, and the bar staff need to take extra steps for every drink, each of those customers doesn't just wait longer for his or her own order, but for every order ahead as well. These people are lining up to give your business money - the last thing you should do is make it difficult for them to do so.

- **Low-cost equipment.** If you can't afford to equip your bar with brand-new reach-in refrigerators, there is another low-cost alternative. Consider keeping a sink full of ice directly beneath the bar top. Have three or four dozen high-turnover bottled beers in the sink at all times. Your staff can refill the "Bud bins" from refrigerated stock whenever there's a slowdown in customer traffic, thereby saving dozens of unnecessary trips to the fridge every hour, not to mention giving your customers faster service.

- **Pre-made mixes.** To save time during their busiest periods, many bars pre-make cocktail mixes. While this is a good plan, be sure not to have these pre-made mixes sitting out in plain view. Ensure your staff don't refill them in the public eye. If your bottom line dictates that you have to use tequila from Peoria, it's best not to advertise the fact when you're charging eight bucks a drink.

The Under-Bar

Your under-bar is the engine of your bar area. If it's designed well, your staff can get from order to delivery in seconds. If it's poorly designed and dysfunctional, your customers and staff could spend a good portion of the night stuck in bar traffic.

- **Focus on the customer.** Employee interaction is the key. The under-bar area should contain everything your staff needs to fill 80 percent of their drink orders without moving a step away from the customer. If your staff aren't able to engage your customers in steady conversation as they're filling their orders, you're not only putting your staff through more work than they need, but you're also making your customers wait too long.

- **Bar layout.** If your staff can work more effectively within a smaller area of the bar, you will be able to fit more staff behind that bar during peak periods, ensuring faster service and higher productivity. Take a fresh look at the bar area and consider what changes you can make to improve productivity.

- **Streamline your workstation.** Many bar-fitting companies sell sink units that include speed racks, jockey boxes, ice sinks and more. They can also replace aged fittings with a minimum of fuss and expense. This will give your staff a compact, efficient workstation from which to maximize their time and effort. Prices vary, but when you consider the time, labor and customer tolerance savings, it's a purchase that will pay for itself many times over. BigTray (www.bigtray.com) can sell you this kind of equipment online or over the phone at 1-800-BIG-TRAY.

Anti-Fatigue Floor Mats

Many commercial bar operators see nonslip matting as a necessity for the floor of the service area. But many managers neglect the obvious advantages a topflight fitted floor mat can bring to their staff and financial bottom line.

- **Added comfort.** Your bartenders are on their feet all day long. A hard floor can wreak havoc on their feet, legs and back. A good antifatigue floor mat can give your staff just enough added comfort to keep sick days and fatigue to a minimum as it absorbs the impact that normally shoots through their joints. An antifatigue mat is like a shock absorber. It provides the much-needed traction your staff requires to work at peak efficiency.

- **Reduce breakages.** Invest in quality bar matting and limit breakages. No member of your staff, no matter how well-trained, is going to go through life without dropping a glass occasionally. It's simply a fact of bar life. If your matting saves half of those dropped glasses from breaking (and your staff from having to clean up shards of broken glass), then the new matting will pay for itself within months.

- **Professional fitting.** Ensure that the mats you purchase are properly fitted to your floor space. There's no point in purchasing safety mats if your staff are continually tripping over them. Companies such as the Sanitary Supply Company (www.sanitarysupplyco.com) can not only sell you quality mats, but they also stock connectors and bevel edges so that you can cut your mat to suit any space. Call 520-624-7436.

When your venue gets busy, does the customer comfort level diminish? Body heat, cigarette smoke, sweat, outside temperature, low oxygen levels and dance-floor fog systems all contribute to making your customers feel less than relaxed. In some cases this will drive them away, never to return. Thankfully, problems such as these can be solved relatively simply:

- **Consider a fresh-air exchange system.** This addition to your existing HVAC (heating, ventilation, air-conditioning) system allows you to draw in a continual flow of fresh air from outside, during times when your venue capacity is at its peak. It can also be adjusted manually to bring in 100 percent fresh air, ensuring minimal customer fatigue from lack of oxygen. In cooler weather it can also substantially cut back on your air-conditioning expenses by using the cooler outside air. Call your local air-conditioning service company and ask them to assist you with these changes.

- **Consider fitting a large fresh-air duct over the dance floor.** A busy dance floor is a prime cause of reduced customer comfort levels. A fresh-air duct can draw in large amounts of fresh air from outside when you decide conditions are getting too clammy. Simply hit a switch behind the bar and the dance floor is blasted with a whoosh of cool air, rejuvenating your dancing patrons and recharging oxygen levels throughout the venue.

- **Nothing is worse than a smoky bar.** Even if you don't have huge crowds and a thumping dance floor, a handful of smokers can quickly dull the atmosphere. Many venues fight this with air-conditioning. However, this can often prove an expensive and ineffective means of combating the problem. A far better way to deal with smoke is with a strong smoke extraction system, which allows your AC system to do its primary job of controlling the temperature far more effectively. Contact KleenAir at www.kleenair-group.com for a full range of smoke extraction products.

Is Your Ice Machine Handling the Pressure?

The ice machine is one of your bar equipment staples. Its working efficiency has an effect on every drink sold. But many bar operators treat ice machines as a mere afterthought. Consider the following:

- **Convenient location.** Your ice machines should be located with convenience in mind. What's convenient to your bar staff matters, not what's convenient to the nearest electrical power outlet and water connection. Ideally, your busiest bar should have its own ice machine located within a few steps from the bar area, if not within it.

- **Install a backup machine in case of breakdown.** During busy periods, or as a go-to option on busy nights, a backup machine is essential. These machines can be expensive, but view the outlay as essentially "ice insurance."

- **Get the capacity right.** The general rule for high-traffic bars is to have an ice-making capacity of three pounds of ice per customer per night. Of course, you won't always use this much, but it's far better to have ice and not need it than need ice and not have it. Remember, ice is cheap.

- **Professional installation.** Even the best ice machines won't work properly if they're installed improperly. The most common cause of ice machine problems is a warm water supply. Also, the route your water pipes travel to get to your ice machine can be the root cause of the problem. Consider having your water lines run through your walk-in cooler or near air-conditioning outlets. By the time the water gets to your ice machine, it will be closer to freezing point.

- **Peak performance.** Ask your ice machine supplier if the water line within the machine runs through the cold sump water discharged by the machine when ice melts. This can help keep your ice machine at peak performance.

- **Adjustable machines.** Some machines can be adjusted to suit the kind of size and shape of ice cube that you prefer to use in your drink creations. As a rule, hollow cubes elliptical ice tend to last longer than regular cubes, though cubes take up more 'drink' space. Don't forget that some people like to eat the ice itself when a drink is done, so tailor your ice to suit.

- **Avoid "clumping."** When ice is poured into an ice bin, it sometimes sticks to itself, forming clumps that are hard to scoop. Combat this by pouring a little club soda from the soda dispensers over the ice.

- **Place a damp bar towel over the opening of the bin.** If you use large bins filled with ice to accommodate busy nights, it will keep the warmer outside air from getting at the ice, thus keeping it from melting for far longer than usual.

Blenders or Slush-Makers?

For high-volume cocktails, sometimes it doesn't pay to hold up the bar while one bartender wrestles with a blender. But will pushing for the pre-made crushed-ice, industrial-strength margarita machine lead your customers to disappointment or higher sales?

- **Investment in a large frozen-drink machine.** Sometimes demand outweighs supply by far too much to consider relying on blenders. A good drink machine holds a lot of alcohol. It can turn a three-minute drink creation into a ten-second pour. These machines also look great - in fact a great-looking frozen drink machine filled with tasty green crushed-ice margarita mix could be the best point-of-sale display your margaritas could have.

- **Quality.** While frozen-drink machines can churn out drinks faster than anything else, sometimes the order calls for something with more quality than quantity. In this situation, you can't beat a great blender. Note: A "great" blender is NEVER a cheap blender. Don't skimp on quality with your blenders - go for industrial-strength steel every time.

- **Durability.** The caution about the construction of your blender extends to what drives it as much as what it's made of. If your blender has a rubber clutch, don't expect it to last when you're cranking out piña coladas, daiquiris and margaritas all night long.

- **Discounts.** Generally, you can get a good discount on a bulk blender purchase - which usually means you have to purchase five machines to qualify. That may be more than you need, but if you get a 20-percent discount in the process, one of those machines is essentially free, so why not take advantage?

Don't Let Your Customers Be Waiters

It costs you plenty to get customers in the door, so when they get there, you sure as heck don't want them walking out again when your host/hostess tells them there will be an hour's wait. Take these steps to ensure that you retain every customer that walks through your door.

- **Create an interesting waiting area.** Some customers just don't want to sit and wait for a table in your bar area. So give them something a little extra to occupy them. Bar games, trivia quizzes, Internet access, a big-screen TV, a substantial jukebox; these are all things that can greatly reduce the time your customers will feel like they waited. It might even bring in more money for your venue in the process.

- **Offer waiting patrons a little something from a passing tray of free appetizers.** It won't hurt your bottom line too much, but it will keep them from giving in to their hunger and going to McDonald's instead. Be sure you don't offer them too much, however, as the object is still to sell them food from your menu! A tray with a nice selection of different foods from your menu can actually be a great advertisement and may even generate increased food sales.

- **Supply your customers with pagers.** Offering waiting customers a page to notify them when their tables are ready is a great alternative to the usual "public address" announcement, or worse, a yell over the din of the crowd. When a table frees up, your host simply dials the waiting group's number and wherever they are in the building (or outside), they know that their table is ready. Contact Bristol Business Machines (www.bristolnf.com) at 709-722-6669 for more information on customer paging systems, or visit your local paging system supplier.

- **"Table manager" software can greatly reduce waiting times.** With these systems, a busperson enters a table number into a wireless pager when the table is cleared, sending a note to the host's screen notifying him or her that the next customers can be seated now. This is far faster and more efficient than having the hostess constantly checking the entire room for cleared tables. Touch2000 Systems (www.restaurant-pos.com) stocks a variety of restaurant management software and even has downloadable demos. Call 203-366-8673.

- **Wireless credit card processing is a reality.** Why make your customers wait for staff to run their cards at the bar when their meal is done? With a wireless system they can run the card right at the table. Newer systems can even print receipts, making bill paying a ten-second process. This allows tables to be cleared faster. These systems can be purchased at www.merchantwarehouse.com. Call 800-941-6557.

- **During long waits, offer waiting customers a free mixed drink.** Allow them to choose from a limited selection of, say, a group of five alternative mixes. A free margarita each effectively means you're losing five shots of tequila, a little lime and a blender full of ice. In real terms, this will cost you a couple of dollars, but your customers will be extremely appreciative when a tray of huge, icy-cold, frosty drinks arrives. They are likely to spend far more in the long run.

- **Keep your customers informed!** Be open and honest. If there'll be a half-hour wait, don't tell them it will be a fifteen-minute wait and hope they don't walk out. Similarly, ensure your staff keeps them updated on how the wait is going so they know they haven't been forgotten. Small things like this make a big difference in the eyes of a waiting customer.

CHAPTER THREE

THE STOCK

A Wide Selection Pays for Itself

What you sell determines how well you sell and whether your new customers will bother returning. Procter & Gamble didn't make billions selling only Crest toothpaste - the name of the game is variety, originality and quality. Picture it; a group of well-dressed customers, clearly from out of town, walks into your bar and orders a round of Courvoisiers. "A what?" asks your bartender. The next sound you hear is the door closing as a potential $120 bar tab walks out the door. You might think that increasing the size of your alcohol selection is money wasted, but stocking a wide variety of goods to sell sure doesn't hurt your local supermarket, and with spirits, liqueurs and even bottled beers being so profitable, it's essential that you capture every customer you can.

- **Impulse sales.** Unlike food, garnishes and juices, which have a short shelf life, spirits, liqueurs and bottled beers have a low spoilage rate. Although certain brands might not sell as quickly as your base drinks, just the fact that they're in plain view will lead to occasional impulse buys. This way, when someone does come into the bar seeking something special, being able to provide what he or she is looking for will impress your potential new customer.

- **Take a "one-brand-at-a-time" approach.** It is definitely possible to go overboard when increasing the variety of your selection. Tying up too much money in inventory is a no-no. Better to try something new every few weeks. Also, for slow-moving lines, let the few bottles you purchased in error run out, and then try something new.

- **Add one product to your selection each time you order from your distributor.** Go for either something that your staff has been asked for once or twice (they'll gladly tell you what people ask for) or a brand that is being offered at a temporarily cheaper rate than normal by your distributor. Investigate special promotions.

- **Try expanding one particular spirit.** Choose vodka or tequila, for example. It will help you market your wider variety of that drink. Customers who favor that particular spirit may be tempted to make a pilgrimage to your establishment for the first time. Stocking 12 tequilas may seem like overkill, but to a tequila drinker, it's heaven.

- **Remove "dead" stock.** If a bottle has been sitting on your shelf for more than nine months, consider it dead stock. Don't let it sit forever; simply get rid of it. Replace it with a new line. A good way to lose stock that isn't moving is to incorporate it in a "cocktail special" or run a special low price on the drink until it's dried up.

- **Smaller bottles.** If you have a few customers who order slower-moving liqueurs and top-shelf spirits, but not enough to go through more than a few bottles per year, think about purchasing those items in smaller bottles - 500ml or 750ml - so that the bottles don't sit on your shelves gathering dust.

Coffee

Starbucks didn't become a multibillion dollar company by catering to a need that doesn't exist. Coffee is big business, and if you're not taking part in the coffee craze, you're missing out on a huge potential revenue stream.

- **Coffee service is an art unto itself.** Serving coffee doesn't mean dishing out Nescafé in paper cups. Just like in bartending, the more exotic and high quality your coffee service is, the more new customers are going to find you - and stay with you. Invest in an espresso coffee machine. If your staff doesn't already know how to use it, train them. Your local yellow pages will list a variety of coffee distributors, all of which can supply you with an espresso machine.

- **Coffee doesn't have to be piping hot to be good.** In fact, there's a whole range of cold coffee products that can have your patrons begging for more. A fresh-brewed, icy-cold, coffee-based cocktail can fill your patrons' desire for a caffeine fix, while still giving them a nice mixed-drink buzz. Simply pour hot coffee into an iced mixing tin, swirl in a liqueur or two and serve to suit.

- **Special glassware.** Coffee drinks should always have their own glassware, if for no other reason than that the heat tends to weaken standard glassware. A heavy 12 or 16-ounce insulated glass will do the trick and, generally, will look very elegant when served. Coffee drinks also look fine in a beer glass, snifter or wine glass. But if you want your customers' hands to remain burn-free, a function-specific coffee glass with a strong side handle is your best bet.

- **Coffee provides a fine nonalcoholic cocktail alternative.** Consider the Strawberry Mocha Float; just take a scoop of ice cream, drop it into the bottom of a nice, thick coffee glass, then blend iced coffee and fresh strawberries. Pour the blender contents onto the center of the ice cream until the glass is half full. Add a dollop of whipped cream, wedge a couple of strawberries onto the side of the glass, and you have a fantastic cocktail creation for a hot day. Mix in some Bailey's to give it a little kick - your customers will be back for more.

Glassware Selection

Choosing your glassware comes down to a lot more than just choosing beer, wine and spirit glasses. Your glassware influences many things, from the size of your servings to the visual appeal of your bar, and can even be an additional promotional effort.

- **Aesthetics.** In a busy bar, there can be hundreds of glasses situated around the room. Spend a little extra on your glassware; those glasses can add an aesthetic quality to your venue. An elegant glass can turn an ordinary cocktail into a work of art. If you add the cost of the glass into the sale price of the drink, you can allow the customer to keep the glass, thereby increasing sales and adding value for the customer.

- **Plastic glassware.** While far cheaper than glass and with a much lower breakage rate, plastic is a lot less attractive, tougher to clean and feels "cheaper" to customers. A good cocktail looks as good as it tastes, and there's nothing better than glass to let the natural colors of the drink shine through.

- **Choose the right glassware for your establishment.** Some glassware looks fantastic, but before you buy three boxes of a certain style, investigate how well the glasses will work for you in practice. Do they stack easily? Are they smooth on the sides and, thus, easier to drop when wet? Will your staff be able to hand-clean them easily, or are they too long and thin? Will your beer glasses produce good foam and maintain it for a long period? Will the style of glass you're about to buy lend itself to multiple uses, or just one style of drink?

- **Are your glasses too exotic?** Spending too much on your glassware brings another kind of problem - that of theft. By all means, be elegant, but keep things in perspective. Also, make sure that the style you're buying is likely to be available over the long-term. If you stock up on a limited line, you might find it impossible to replace those glasses at a later date when you've had a few breakages.

- **Test tubes can make a great novelty cocktail.** They can also make a great cut-price special. Test tubes can be used for Jell-O shots for added profitability. Most glassware suppliers can sell you test tubes and serving racks at a good price. But do take into account that they are hard to clean and that they are prone to theft. Price accordingly. Contact your glassware supplier for more details, or talk to Armsco (www.armsco.com) by calling 602-957-2142.

- **Yard-of-ale.** Beer in yard-glasses can be a huge seller depending on your crowd. Finishing a yard-glass is often seen as a rite of passage, so if you get a young crowd or large groups, make sure you stock a number of yard-glasses. If you really want to increase profitability and the appeal of the drink, build the cost of the glass into the price and give it away with each sale.

Mix Your Beers — Boost Your Sales!

In Canadian, European and Australian bars, it's long been a tradition to mix-and-match beer types. Customers today have varying tastes, and sometimes the types of beers supplied on the domestic market don't suit every palette. For that reason, many bars have started to see the logic in offering blends of different beers as a means of boosting beer sales. For example:

- **The Black and Tan.** Mix Guinness with any traditional amber ale. The two beers have very different textures and densities and, thus, you can layer the Guinness over the other beer, creating a dramatic appearance and a unique flavor. When the glass is tilted, the two levels mix at the rim of the glass, but when set down again, the layers stay intact.

- **The Half and Half.** This is a mixture of pilsner and bitter. The pilsner takes the edge off the bitter and the bitter gives the pilsner a kick. The result is a great "mid-range" beer to suit a variety of tastes. Along similar lines is the Rock 'n Bock, made with Rolling Rock and any kind of bock ale. Blend Guinness and honey lager to create a Bumble Bee, or Guinness and Foster's Lager if you'd prefer a Koala Bear.

- **Shandy.** This mixture of beer with a dash of club soda (or 7-Up) was more popular before the growth of light beer as a commercial product. Its unique flavor, however, still means it has a place in the hearts of many who like the taste of beer, but prefer it to be a little softer to the palette. It also goes down like a dream on a hot day. Use lemon-lime and soda, instead, to make a Lemon Top, ginger ale to make a Shandy Gaff, or lime to make a Lager & Lime. In Australia, a "Fifty" is a mix of full strength and light beer.

- **Be adventurous.** Sometimes a non-beer additive can turn a common beer into a taste explosion. Take, for example, the Dr. Pepper, made by setting a shot glass of amaretto into a mug of beer - guaranteed to shake the head of any beer drinker. Throw in a shot of rum to give it a deeper kick: the Dr. Pepper from Hell. Mixing any beer with tomato juice will give you a Red Eye, which, when mixed into a Bloody Mary, makes a great "hair of the dog that bit you."

- **The Black Velvet is a timeless creation and great for Sunday brunch.** A blend of Guinness and chilled champagne, it's said that it's like being "hit in the head with a brick wrapped in a velvet cloth." Replacing the champagne with cider will give you a Black Velveteen, which is a nice economic alternative.

- **Some beer creations can be darn scary - until you try them.** Take for example the Bloody Bastard, a blend of Bass Ale, Bloody Mary, horseradish and a peeled shrimp garnish. But even that pales in comparison to the Oyster Shooter: a mix of Tabasco sauce, beer, horseradish and a raw oyster, served in a chilled glass.

Glassware Care

Many factors can lead to glassware breakage, the most obvious being accidental dropping of said glassware by your staff and customers. Happily, many of the other factors that lead to breakage can be prevented, or at the least lessened, if you know what to look out for. Consider the following:

- **Thermal changes.** Glass retains heat, so when you take a glass out of the washer, it takes time for that glass to cool down to room temperature.

Consequently, if you throw ice and a cold drink in the glass while it's still hot, the sudden change in temperature will likely cause the glass to develop tiny cracks and weak spots. Combat this potential problem by ensuring that all glasses are allowed to cool sufficiently before use.

- **Weakening through impact.** Your glasses will generally take a pounding in the course of the day. Provide your bar staff with nonmetal ice scoops, and ensure they never use the glass itself as an ice scoop.

- **Make sure that your glass racks fit the shape of your glasses.** You don't want your glasses to rattle around, either during the machine-washing process or when they're being moved about the bar.

- **Avoid stacking.** Ensure your glass-collecting staff don't stack too many glasses on top of one another as they clear tables. Your glasses may be designed to stack into one another, but when you stack them 20 high, the bottom glass is going to take a dangerous level of stress and, in all likelihood, will weaken, if not break.

- **Observe your glass stock.** Over time any glass will accumulate scratches and cracks, even chips. The temptation is to keep using these glasses until they're totally unusable. Don't. This practice can hurt your bottom line more than help it. When you serve a drink in a glass that cracks, you have to replace the drink, not to mention hope that the cracking doesn't take place when your customer has the glass to his or her lips.

- **Rotate your stock regularly.** If a glass looks like it has been around for a while, put it away as emergency stock for a busy night, or throw it out altogether. You might spend a little extra on glassware in the process, but you'll avoid many of the broken glass incidents that could conceivably cost you thousands when somebody becomes injured.

Vodka Ethics

A lot of drinkers see spirits as spirits and wouldn't know a good scotch whisky if it jumped out of their glass and bit them on the side of the face. A greater number of customers, however, are capable of pointing out a quality spirit and have strong views on how they want their drink to be prepared. Vodka drinkers are amongst the most discerning around. It pays, therefore, to follow a few simple rules when dealing with this spirit:

- **Vodka won't freeze.** Place your non-well vodkas in a fridge so that those who order it without a mixer can get the best possible experience. Vodka is best served icy cold, and though ice will help, not all vodka drinkers want their spirit diluted this way.

- **An attractive display.** To make sure that your refrigerated vodka products aren't overlooked by your customers, leave a bottle of every brand up on your bottle display. It doesn't have to be full;

it could contain water if you don't want stock sitting around, or you can even leave it up there empty. It is important, however, to let customers know that you stock good brands, even if the bottle you serve from is in cold storage.

- **Neat vodka.** If some of your customers enjoy drinking neat vodka, consider chilling a few glasses in the same freezer so that they're well frosted when those customers place their orders. A little consideration like this may turn a passing vodka connoisseur into a regular customer.

Reducing Spoilage

Beer, spirits and liqueurs don't have an indefinite shelf life, and while this isn't news to most bar managers, it's certainly unknown to a lot of bar staff. Follow these simple rules to ensure that your staff is doing all it can to turn over your stock:

- **All new stock should be put in the back of fridges.** It's a temptation, especially during busy periods, to replace stock in fridges by just filling the holes. But in doing this, staff could be consigning perishable bottled beers to many months in the back of the fridge. The difference in taste between a fresh bottle of beer and one that's four months old is substantial. Set a day every week when all the fridge stock is taken out and rotated before the bar opens.

- **Kegs are perishable.** Long-term exposure to the gases used to push beer through the lines can easily turn a keg bad. When closing for a few days over Christmas or on public holidays, be sure to clear your lines and de-gas all kegs so as to keep the beer as pure as possible.

- **Slow sellers.** If certain draft beers sell slower than others, investigate whether your distributor deals in smaller-keg sizes to ensure that your beer remains fresh.

- **Avoid warm, foamy beer.** If a beer line is unused for a period, the entire line of beer can become warm and foamy. This will mean that in pouring one beer, you'll be wasting the equivalent of three just waiting for the line to get back to normal. Running the last few feet of the beer lines through a cooling unit is a good way to reduce waste in slow draft lines. Establishing costs can be recouped in reduced waste within months.

- **Monitor slow-moving liqueurs.** Slow movers with free-pouring spouts can sometimes get a little disgusting towards the end of the bottle if not washed regularly. Also, the fresh air that comes in through a free-pourer can make certain liqueurs turn sludgy, or even let bugs into the bottle. Ensure that slow-moving liqueurs are fitted with controlled pourers that keep the bottle relatively airtight. Alternatively, use jiggers and keep the bottle tops attached.

- **Cut garnishes do not keep well.** Have the bar staff cut garnishes as they go to reduce waste. Make certain that your customers get the freshest garnishes possible.

Nonalcoholic Drinks

In these enlightened times, not everyone likes to have a "vice," and a growing number of people choose not to drink. But just as Las Vegas caters to non-gamblers, a bar that caters to non-drinkers can turn a huge increase in numbers. Here's how.

- **Dedicate a portion of your cocktail menu to nonalcoholic drinks.** It's easy to make an exotic creation full of color and flavor without filling it full of rum. Utilizing tea, coffee, juices, soda, sherbet, ice cream and yogurt, it doesn't take much to come up with some breathtaking creations that can have non-drinkers feeling at home - and paying liquor prices - while their friends party the night away.

- **Stock a selection of fresh-squeezed juices.** It doesn't have to mean you're going "up-market." Most bar operations have plenty of oranges, strawberries, apples, etc., for the making of cocktails and the cutting of garnishes. Using these items and more to provide a selection of exotic juices will not only bring in more early-morning and lunchtime traffic, it will also widen your cocktail possibilities.

- **Smart drinks and energy drinks are big business!** Long popular in Europe, energy drinks have caught on like wildfire in North America, of late. Red Bull is an energy drink in a can that is going through the roof in sales the last few years, and juice bar chains like Jamba Juice are springing up everywhere. These places not only serve fresh-squeezed fruit-juice creations, but they also allow customers to add "shots" of vitamins, minerals, antioxidants and more, to give them energy, boost immunity, beat a hangover - whatever is desired. These are big with the after-club crowd, so they're a great potential morning-business boost.

- **Sport drinks.** These drinks are becoming increasingly popular. Nowadays, a growing number of establishments are working them into new drink creations. Stocking Gatorade might be a great move if you're close to a gym or in a warm climate. When mixed with other drinks, it can provide a boost to people sweating up a storm on the dance floor.

CHAPTER FOUR

THE STAFF

Finding the Best Possible Staff

Asuccessful bar operation depends on people more than anything - the people coming into your bar and the people behind it. How you treat your staff, how you find them, how you train them and how they work are keys factor in hospitality success. Many bar managers find that one of the most difficult tasks in their job is finding the right people to join their staff. If you want the best possible employees (and you shouldn't want anything less), these rules might assist you in your search:

- **Headhunt.** If you want simply to fill a handful of roster slots with physically able bodies, classified ads may be a fine option. Classified ads will certainly bring you applicants. However, the best hospitality people are generally not unemployed; they're already working for your competition. Take a look around the better local establishments. If you see someone worth headhunting, make him or her an offer.

- **Ask your existing staff.** They can be a great source of new staff; they usually know plenty of industry colleagues that would be a nice fit in your bar, and though you don't want to form "cliques," a personal reference from someone you respect sure as heck beats a cattle call.

- **Offer a finder's fee.** If someone working for you brings in a new employee that stays with you past a probationary period, a $75 bonus will get your existing people thinking hard about staffing possibilities.

- **Keep applications on file!** If someone walks in the door and asks for a job when none has been advertised, you can bet they already know and like your establishment and truly want to work there. Motivated souls such as these make prime pickings, so don't disregard their applications - keep them and get in touch when you need to.

- **Time is money.** Don't waste too much of it by interviewing everyone who applies to you. If an applicant isn't to your initial liking, thank him or her for the application and move on to someone who is.

- **The need to earn.** It's traditionally thought that the more stabilizing factors there are in a person's life, such as being a student, having a mortgage or being married with children, the less likely that person will be to leave suddenly or jeopardize his or her job through tardiness.

- **What are you looking for exactly?** Different roles require different skills. While not every position requires abundant experience, every position does require a mix of stability, intelligence, personality, honesty and a willingness to work. If an inexperienced applicant shows these qualities, look past any lack of skills and make an investment in a quality human being with training.

- **Every employee is a reflection of your corporate personality.** It's important that employees view every customer as a potential friend, not an irritation. Certain people can light up a room with a smile, and if you can find two or three of those people, your customers will be back.

- **Never interview an applicant who has just made his or her application.** Let him or her show enthusiasm when you call about an interview at a later date. If the applicant can't make it or doesn't show up, you're better off without.

- **Ask the right questions.** If you want to be sure you have all the information you require from each person, put together a list of questions in advance. This will allow you to get comfortable, focus on the answers and stay on target.

- **Don't be afraid to ask for a demonstration.** If a prospective bartender has trouble uncorking a bottle of wine or mixing a good martini, it's better that you find out ahead of time.

How Do You Test for Honesty?

Dishonest employees are not always going to make themselves obvious. Sometimes the person with the biggest smile has something even bigger to hide. When hiring your staff, how can you go about discovering who is to be trusted and who should be shown the doors?

- **Background check.** This might seem a draconian tactic to determine if your potential employees are who they say they are. You can run a check on your prospective staff online through an outfit like US Search (www.ussearch.com), who will take the person's details and run a check on credentials for only $59.95 - $99.95 for a criminal background check. The results of these searches can, in most cases, be e-mailed to you within 24 hours, with full details taking up to seven days.

- **References.** Thorough checking of all references is a must, especially for a person interviewing for a position of trust. Call every company listed on the employee's resume and be sure to ask the correct questions: Why did the person leave? How long was she there? What position did he hold? Would the company gladly take him back if given the opportunity?

- **Credit check.** If prospective employees will be in a position where they're exposed to a large amount of money, it may be prudent to run a credit check before you employ them.

- **Sometimes the simplest approach is the best.**
  Why not just ask potential employees if they've
  ever taken something that wasn't theirs? Watch
  their body language when you ask the question.
  Do they blush? Do they avert their eyes? Do they
  fidget? Do they nod their head, as they say "no"?

A Few Important "Integrity" Questions Will Tell You a Lot About a Person

For the most part, a person who will tell the truth
and risk putting himself in a negative light is far
more impressive than someone who gives you the
answer he thinks you want to hear. Ask your job
applicants these simple but important questions and
take note of the response itself, but also the way the
response is delivered. A note of caution: labor laws
are constantly changing. Some questions may not be
permissible by either state or federal law. Visit
www.dol.gov for the latest in federal law regulations,
as well as your state's Department of Labor Web site.

- **Has your new employee ever been in trouble
  with the law?** A "yes" answer doesn't
  necessarily mean you're dealing with a criminal,
  but it's important that you get both the
  applicant's and the police's side of the story.
  Forewarned is forearmed.

- **Has the applicant ever been accused, rightly
  or wrongly, of theft or fraud?** Again, a "yes"
  answer doesn't necessarily mean the person in
  question is dishonest. In fact, a person who will
  come clean about a questionable episode in his
  or her life should be commended for this

honesty, especially if he or she can fully explain the incident.

- **"A fellow bartender is scamming the bar and you know about it. What do you do?"** Hypothetical questions like these are great ways to explore how a potential employee thinks and how he or she will act in a crunch.

- **Ask the applicant to relate an incident where someone he or she knows showed extreme integrity and honesty.** When she's done, ask the person if she thinks she would do the same thing in the same situation. A "no" answer is just fine, as it's an honest response. If you're looking for honesty from a new employee, a real response is far better than a sales pitch.

Security Staff

Knowing when and how to recruit security staff is an important part of any popular bar operation. Should you hire your own or deal with a security firm? If you hire your own people, what rules do you set for them? How do you avoid getting sued if someone is removed forcibly? Many venues utilize outside security firms to provide security on busy nights, and most do so as a means of simplifying their security needs and reducing liability issues. But an outside contractor doesn't always make things easier:

- **Outside contractors.** This means you don't need to concern yourself with compensation, holidays, sick days, wages, etc. However, it also means that your level of control over the standard and selection of those who work at your venue is reduced. Also, with security firms costing more per hour than individual contractors or staff, your bottom line can suffer. Consider hiring one or two of your own staff who you can use on regularly busy nights and filling in any gaps with contractors that may come up.

- **In-house employees.** While harder to find, train, and do background checks on, they are usually more loyal and tend to stay longer than contractors. If you want to have complete control over how your security behaves, how they deal with customers and their loyalty to the company, there can be no better way to work than to simply employ the best people you can find.

- **Security personnel.** Hiring security and calling them independent contractors to avoid liability and payroll taxes is a tactic some bar operators employ to make the process simpler and cheaper. But this can bring more problems than it solves. If your security "contractor" does injure someone when removing him or her from the premises, are you confident that your "contractor" won't claim she is an employee? Do you need that kind of a fight?

- **Rules.** Security guards need ironclad rules of engagement that dictate what they can and cannot do. Ensure that rules are in place that every security employee knows and signs. So, if there is a liability problem down the road, you can point out that your rules were broken and that you were not in any way negligent in your duty of care to the client.

- **ALWAYS do a background check on your potential security staff.** It may cost a little and extend the hiring process, but if you don't want a 300-pound cocaine addict to be throwing your customers around a back alley, you'll want to make sure you're not hiring any 300-pound cocaine addicts.

- **Attorney involvement.** Talk to your lawyer about drawing up any and all papers you'll need to ensure that your organization is completely covered and doing everything it can to ensure your security staff behave responsibly. Spending a hundred bucks today on legal fees can save you thousands down the road. Similarly, check with your insurance company to confirm your legal liability responsibilities to your security staff.

- **Subcontracting security staff is a legitimate means of filling a need.** This works if you really don't have the time to micromanage your security concerns, or to fill in during times when your regular staff is unavailable or inadequate in number. You can subcontract individuals as long as you give them a Form 1099 for any cash paid over the $600 mark; this will, in turn, keep your workers' compensation bill down.

- **Equip your security staff for their job.** Spotting fake IDs isn't always easy. If you have 200 people waiting to go through your door, your security staff can't spend five minutes with every person, but there are tools available that can help. An electronic ID-checking unit will read the magnetic strip on any state driver license, verify that the license is valid, and display the holder's exact age - not to mention point out if the document is a fake or has been tampered with. These systems are small, inexpensive to purchase and limit the chance that your staff will let in an underage drinker. Talk to Intelli-Check (www.intellicheck.com) by calling 800 444-9542.

Do Your Bartenders Create Regulars?

The bar business is not, as many people think, a service industry. Of course, it's part service industry, but it's also very important not to forget that it's also an entertainment industry. Do your bartenders entertain your customers while they are serving them?

- **Every customer is an asset to your business.** Just as you wouldn't throw chairs and tables away after one use, so too should you do everything in your power to make sure that every customer comes back again and again. Your staff must know that this is your goal. They must realize that they're the front-line weapons in the battle for customer retention.

- **Customer needs.** Every staff member, from host to bartender to manager, should be able to handle any customer's needs. If a hostess walks past a table that obviously needs clearing without lifting a finger, how do you think that will leave those customers feeling about the service standard in your bar?

- **People seated at the bar.** They should be treated like old friends by your bar staff, at least when they first sit down. But just as it's important to engage customers in conversation when they're happy to talk, it's also important to leave them alone when they don't. A good bartender reads the client's mood.

- **Flair bartending is all the rage.** Bartenders who consider their job to be more than a temporary source of income see themselves as the next Tom Cruise in the movie *Cocktail.* While putting on a show for the customers is a great way to entertain them, putting on a bad show is not. If your staff want to sling bottles and glasses around the bar in style, make sure they work within their limitations and save the practicing for after-hours.

- **Staff incentives.** Some bar operators give incentives to their bar staff to stay around after their shifts and get to know the customers. Discounted drinks and food are not only a relatively cost-effective way to have your staff spend their free time at work, but these methods also help convince them to bring their own friends and turn your bar into their regular watering hole.

Scams to Watch For

Employees can very easily fall into a habit of scamming their employers, and if you're not careful, you can be caught out for thousands of dollars, not to mention disgruntled customers. Keep an eye out for these 14 favorites:

- **The substitute.** An employee buys his own bottle of a fast-moving spirit, brings it in at the start of the shift, and over the course of the night substitutes his own for the bar's bottle. Every time he sells a shot of this product, he then simply pockets the money, thus earning a large profit on his own alcohol while your stock stands still. While these people are not thieving your stock per se, they're thieving your business, so ensure you stamp or mark all of your spirit and liqueur bottles; check the empties regularly, and keep employee bags away from the bar and stockroom areas.

- **The short-pour.** Your bartender short-pours every shot of a particular fast-selling spirit by between 25 and 50 percent, keeps note of how many shots she's sold from the bottle and when she's sold the number of shots that usually come from the bottle, she pockets the money from the remaining shots. Make sure that you check register receipts against the bottles used, and if possible, you use a computer-controlled pouring system, to take the opportunity to scam out of the employee's hands.

- **The "00."** Some registers can be opened with the press of just one button or from entering in a total of $0.00. Unbeknownst to some bar operators, this is the number-one means of rip-offs by staff. A customer buys a beer and gives the bartender a fiver. "Keep the change," says the customer as he walks off, so the employee hits the "register open" button, puts in the five-dollar bill and takes out five dollars in coins and singles for his or her pocket or tip jar. How do you avoid this scam? Remove that button. Your cash register provider can do this with no problem at all, and if a customer needs change in the future, your bartender simply asks him to wait for another sale to take place. Or even better, provide change machines.

- **Bogus breakage.** Oops! A full vodka bottle hits the floor and the bar loses, big time. But did it really hit the floor? You might have a breakage bucket in which your staff are to put any broken bottles to show that they actually broke, but how do you know that the contents weren't poured into a hip flask beforehand? Or worse, that the contents were sold and the proceeds pocketed? The answer is simple: start a "you break it, you pay for it" rule. Of course, you don't need to enforce this rule if you don't think people are taking advantage, but it will stop the thieves.

- **Wasted waste.** "The beer lines were a little gassy today." Well, that might explain the two gallons of beer waste in the drip trays - but does it really? Pocketing the money for a draft beer and pouring a glass of water into the drip tray is an age-old scam and very hard to detect. Make sure your staff keep measurements of any beer waste and keep track of who wastes what. In time, any trends should become apparent, and even if certain staff members aren't crooked, you'll be able to tell very easily if they need lessons at pouring beer.

- **The backhander.** Your security staff might not feel that taking ten bucks to let someone into the front of the line is wrong, but at the end of the night, when the person who paid that ten bucks has to go home because she's out of cash, it's your potential bottom line that suffers. To combat this, simply ask someone you know to go to the door and offer a kickback to jump the line. If the kickback is accepted, you need a new security guard.

- **The over-charger.** Your bartender either rings up a price higher than what you've set for a drink or charges regular prices but rings up "Happy Hour" prices, pocketing the difference. To combat this, ensure that cash register tapes are changed at the end of every shift and the bartender explains any "Happy Hour" discounts. Likewise, ensure that all drink prices are posted clearly for your customers so that they can identify an overcharge.

- **The over-pourer.** This bartender simply pours more than he or she needs to and hopes for a hefty tip. Keep an eye on your inventory, and this one should be easy to spot.

- **Rounding up rounds.** Bartenders tally up a round of drinks as a "total price," rather than as separate items. This makes it easier to inflate that price without it being noticed by the customers. They then pocket the difference when they ring it up. To combat this possibility, keep drink prices clearly posted behind the bar or on table menus.

- **The "soft" scam.** Your bartender simply neglects to charge for the mixer component of a drink, thus peeling a small bonus for every mixed drink he or she sells. This should be easy to spot if you check register ribbons, but if you don't, your staff can make a fortune.

- **The "padded" tab.** When your customers run a tab, the bartender pencils in an inflated total, takes the money from the customer, then later erases it, replacing it with a correct total. Removing pencils from behind the bar and telling your staff that they must use pens is the best way to fight this one.

- **The substituted cash register tape.** This ingenious little plan involves the bartender leasing a cash register just like yours and bringing in his or her own prepared cash register tape, substituting it for the real tape and pocketing the cash difference. Essentially, if you keep bartenders from "Z"ing their own tapes, you'll prevent this from being possible.

- **The refund.** This is a simple, small-time scam where the bartender claims that a discrepancy in his or her takings was refunded to a customer for money lost in faulty vending machines or gaming equipment. Have any customer seeking a refund fill in a small claim form, with phone number and ID details included, and this shouldn't be an issue. Most customers won't mind doing this if they have a legitimate refund claim.

- **The jigger switch.** The bartender brings in his or her own shot glass that seems identical to your normal barware, but is actually smaller. After several short measures, the bartender can start pocketing money without the inventory showing a shortage. Fight this by clearly marking your pouring measures and doing regular checks of your bar equipment.

Common Excuses for Theft

Why do they do it? Your bar is a good place to work; you're a decent boss - you pay above-average wages - why does your staff feel the need to break the law? Put simply, human nature is to take something for nothing when the chance arises. An informed bar manager is in a far better position to fight losses from theft.

- **Greed.** Theft isn't always about needing a little something extra to pay the bills; some employees just plain old enjoy beating the system. The thrill of getting a sneaky ten bucks is far more important to these people than the actual dollar value.

- **Rationalizing criminal behavior.** "I didn't think it was hurting anybody," is a terrible excuse, but you'll hear it again and again. A little fiddle here and there is seen, in some employees' minds, as not doing anyone any harm.

- **Tip boosting.** Some employees feel that if a customer isn't doing his or her part by leaving a reasonable tip, then turnabouts is fair play. Tips make up a significant part of any bartender's pay, and when the tips are low, they try to make up the difference in other ways.

- **Resentment.** People don't always take orders, or discipline, well and sometimes members of staff who feel "picked on" will strike out by "getting even" with the manager or the venue that they feel has wronged them.

- **"It was there."** Human beings can be impulsive creatures, and sometimes leaving the opportunity for a staff member to defraud the system is all the person in question needs to kick into action: "I don't know what came over me!"

Theft-Reduction Procedures

More often than not, scams and thievery can be detected and/or prevented relatively easily. Strict enforcement of all employee rules is a must and vigorous prosecution of any offenders is essential. Employees must be made clearly aware of the dire consequences of flouting the house rules - every detail must be addressed.

- **Have a manager total the cash at the end of a bar shift.** While the bartenders may feel distrusted, you can always point out that the rule is in place to protect honest staff.

- **House rules.** All new members of staff should be required to sign a confirmation that they have read the house rules, fully understand the implications involved and agree to follow the rules to the letter.

- **No drinking on duty.** Prohibit all bartenders from drinking while on duty. Also, strictly regulate off-duty drinking. Off-duty drinking can see fellow bar staff overpouring, giving away free drinks or undercharging their colleagues, and while staff should be encouraged to socialize with patrons after hours, this should be closely watched.

- **Bartenders should not be involved in the stock-taking and inventory-counting process.** Nor should they be involved in receiving, ordering or issuing inventory. It might be a painful process, but this really should be a management-only function.

- **High-value inventory.** Strictly enforce all security procedures for liquor, wine, beer, spirits and any other high-value inventory. Only key personnel should have access to storage areas, and everything that comes out should be duly noted.

- **Require bartenders to record post-shift bar-par readings.** This refers to the number of bottles left in fridges and behind the bar after a shift has ended. Engage in spot-checking of this count to ensure that no thieving is taking place.

- **Prohibit the practice of recording more than one transaction per drink ticket.** If your bartenders are allowed to use a "running" ticket, they can easily neglect to record all the drinks they have actually sold and pocket the difference.

- **Strictly enforce voiding procedures.** If an amount is rung up on the register, the bartender should not be allowed to void it without management approval.

CHAPTER FIVE

THE SERVING

Establishing House Drink Recipes

A bartender makes a good drink with originality, panache, speed and skill - but a great drink starts with the boss. You determine the drink menu, you determine the recipes to be used and you set the price and make the rules. Your staff just follows your lead. In many bars, it's left to individual members of staff to know the "standard" formulas for cocktails and mixed drinks. Everyone is supposed to know that a Tequila Sunrise has one shot of tequila, right? Or is it two? Maybe it's a shot and a half... Profits are too hard won to just throw away alcohol when your staff crosses their wires about your drink recipes. Some easy steps to ensuring standardization of your house recipes include:

- **Recipe lists.** Make sure when you take on new staff they receive detailed recipe lists to take home and look over before they start their first shift. It doesn't cost you a lot to photocopy a few pages of text and give them to your staff, so make sure there's no excuse for them not to know as much as they can before they start mixing on your dime.

- **Recipes on display.** Ensure that there are either laminated index cards or recipes listed

behind the bar at all times so that any member
of staff - even emergency fill-ins and temps - can
see exactly what is needed to prepare each drink
- no more, no less. Below is an example of a
recipe card and the information it should
contain:

ITEM _____

INGREDIENTS:	PROCEDURE:	GLASS:
_____	_____	_____
_____	_____	_____
_____	_____	_____
_____	_____	**GARNISH:**
_____	_____	_____
_____	_____	_____
_____	_____	_____
_____	_____	_____
_____	_____	_____
_____	_____	_____

ITEM _____

INGREDIENTS:	PROCEDURE:	GLASS:
_____	_____	_____
_____	_____	_____
_____	_____	_____
_____	_____	**GARNISH:**
_____	_____	_____
_____	_____	_____
_____	_____	_____
_____	_____	_____
_____	_____	_____
_____	_____	_____

- **Cocktail menus.** When you leave cocktail menus on tables, make sure that each one shows exactly what is in the drink - not just the ingredients, but the ounce amounts of each. This will not only serve as a more informative drink menu to your customers, but will also allow them to more accurately measure what they've consumed over the course of the night.

- **Premium ingredients.** If you use premium or middle-shelf ingredients in your cocktails, make sure that your cocktail menus make a point of that fact by showing the brands used. There's no point in hiding the fact that your base spirits and liqueurs are of a higher quality than those of your competition, especially because your liquor distributor might chip in for some of the cost of printing if they're being marketed in your literature in this fashion.

- **Accuracy.** Make certain that the cocktail and mixed-drink recipes give a clear indication of what glass is to be used, what garnish should be used, for how long and on what setting any blended drink should be blended and what brands of alcohol should be used for their creation. If you leave anything out, you can bet someone will get it wrong - and with alarming regularity.

- **Bartending recipe computer programs.** For example, Interworlds Software's "BarBack for Windows" can tell your staff how to create a drink even if a customer asks for something ridiculously obscure. BarBack includes over 10,000 different drink recipes, as well as information on glassware, ingredients, mixing methods and garnishes. Rather than taking away from the skills of your staff, insightful programs such as these actually complement their skills to ensure your customers get exactly what they want in the quickest possible time. BarBack can be downloaded at http://hoflink.com/~pknorr/barback.

Mixed Drink Tips

Making a good mixed drink isn't always a matter of A + B = C. In fact, there are numerous small details that can contribute to turning your creation into something just that little bit better than the norm and, more still, that can help you keep your ingredients at peak freshness and productivity. Consider the following:

- **Champagne wastage.** Many mixed drinks require champagne or sparkling white wine as an ingredient. Opening a fresh bottle for one drink can be wasteful. Consider purchasing a champagne bottle resealer for your bar, and make sure your bar staff knows how to use it.

- **Keep champagne fresh.** If you have a steady flow of champagne drinks in your bar, just drop the handle of a metal spoon into the top of the champagne bottle and put it back in the fridge. This will keep the sparkle in your champagne for up to 12 hours.

- **Is fresh-squeezed orange and lemon juice a selling feature of your cocktail menu?** If so, you should know that you'll get a lot more juice from lemons and oranges if you soak them in warm water for a while before juicing them.

- **Stir, don't shake.** When a mixed drink consists of clear liquids and/or carbonated beverages, stir it - don't shake it. You don't want your clear liquids to bruise, nor your bubbles to go flat, and shaking the concoction guarantees both will happen.

- **"Difficult ingredients."** Mixed drinks containing juices, sugar, eggs, cream, milk, or any other difficult-to-mix ingredient should be shaken - and shaken like crazy. Don't just give the contents a three-second rock around the mixer; give 'em heck!

- **Adding eggs.** When you shake a drink that requires an egg, add an ice cube to the shaker. This will help break up the egg and allow it to blend into the drink more easily.

- **Prevent dripping.** When serving wine or champagne from the bottle, a clean piece of wax paper rubbed along the rim of the bottle will prevent any dripping when you pour.

Glass-Handling Rules

All too often, bar staff think of glasses as disposable partyware and all but ignore the fundamental rules of handling drink service equipment. Make your bar staff aware of the following, or you could find yourself in hot water down the road when someone complains of an injury:

- **Never, ever, use glasses as ice scoops.** A tiny chip of glass falling into your ice bin can cause a great deal of injury, and bar glassware certainly isn't designed to shovel rocks of ice. Along the same lines, any time a glass breaks in or near an ice bin, the entire ice bin needs to be emptied and the contents disposed of before it can be used in the preparation of another drink.

- **Staff should never touch the upper half of a glass in the act of serving a drink.** It's unhygienic; it looks terrible to the customer; and the glass will be much more susceptible to breakage if it's being handled regularly in this manner.

- **Stemmed glasses.** They're far more susceptible to breakage than most other types of glasses - not to mention usually more expensive. Make sure that all staff take extra care in the handling of these items, perhaps even to the point of washing them by hand.

- **Inspect.** All glasses need to be inspected, if only briefly, before they're used in a drink order. A lipstick smudge, chip, crack or remnants of a previous drink are not only off-putting to a customer, but they're also hazardous to the customer's health.

Quality Mixed Drinks

The difference between a good and great martini is very small, but very important. The quality of your cocktail menu should be of paramount importance to you. The methods by which those cocktails are prepared should be a point of pride for all concerned.

- **Presentation.** The color and presentation of any exotic mixed drink is key, and by adjusting the amounts of key ingredients, the bartender can not only change the color of a drink, but can also adapt it to suit any taste. Impress the customers by asking how they like their drinks mixed. Would he like it sweet? Does she like it dry? Maybe a little easy on a key ingredient? Often they'll have no preference, but in asking you'll impress the finicky customer.

- **The process of drink creation can be as important as the drink itself.** A little showmanship in the preparation of a drink may slow the process down a touch. Also, if the performance is good and the bartender shows personality, your customers might not mind a little longer wait.

- **Garnishes.** Maraschino cherries, olives, a sprig of mint, a stick of celery, banana, lemon, lime, all carefully prepared, an investment in fridge space, and a bartender who is quick with a paring knife - they can all set your mixed drinks off with a sparkle. The right garnish is as important as the right ingredients.

- **Novelty glassware.** Most bars consider glassware as merely a vessel in which to serve drinks, but the clever operators see that using exotic and novelty glassware and building the cost of the glass into the drink price can bring customers flocking to that drink in order to get the free glass.

Servers Don't Have to Be Boring

A few subtle changes can see your serving staff taken from trusty employees to stars of the bar. Quite often, in fact, the impression your servers leave will be the lasting impression customers take away from their experience at your bar.

- **Serving staff should always see themselves as far more than just drink servers.** In fact, the members of your serving staff are the best positioned to read the mood of the room, point out any glitches in the customer experience, ensure that the bar staff are on their toes and that your patrons get what they need, when they need it. Let your serving people know that they control the floor and that if something is amiss, it's their job to either take care of it or let you know.

- **Professionals.** A good crew of truly professional serving staff is well worth finding and, even more, worth keeping. An average server can handle up to two tables' orders at a time, but many pros can take eight tables of orders at a time - or more! Keep an eye on your servers and always encourage them, through positive encouragement and financial incentives, to expand their skills.

- **Don't skimp in wages or incentives for the best servers.** A few extra bucks an hour for a top-notch server can translate to entire tables of customers getting in an extra round or two of drinks before it's time to go home, which makes you more money, not less.

- **Neon trays.** Some bars have recently discovered a novel way of serving drinks to their customers: glowing neon trays. These establishments utilize black lights throughout the bar, and as a result, the glowing trays make servers far easier to spot. Order them from Glo-Tray at 203-226-3090.

The Service Bar

Aservice bar is an area of the bar dedicated to the drinks servers only. If designed well it can greatly improve the flow of drinks from the bar to the customers. Alternately, if your service bar is not designed well, it can add yet another delay in an already-crowded process. When setting up a service bar, the things that should be considering are:

- **Layout.** Will your staff need to make a long trip, past waiting customers, to get to your drinks server? Placing the service area off to the side of the bar might seem like a good plan when the bar is empty, but when it's full, a drinks server who has to yell to be heard is a disgruntled drinks server - and a frequently delayed one.

- **Drinks station.** Is everything the bartender needs to prepare drinks positioned within six feet (a step and a reach) from a drink preparation area? If it isn't, you're only adding waiting time, opportunity for spillage and even waste to the drinks serving process.

- **How far do your drinks servers have to travel to reach your customers?** Do you seriously expect your server to negotiate a heavy crowd with 12 drinks on his or her tray and not encounter spillage? Clear the way. Improve not just your server's efficiency but also customer traffic flow.

- **Service bar communication.** If you have a bartender or bar devoted purely to drinks service, consider providing your servers with radio headsets that will allow them to communicate a drinks order to the bar from the floor. This simple move can save your servers from making literally hundreds of trips across the floor a night and can slash service times considerably.

Dealing with Intoxicated Customers

The biggest dilemma facing a bar operation is that while the law says you can't allow your customers to get too drunk, your customers are inevitably looking to do just that when they walk into your establishment. Working within the law is very important if you're going to keep your license. But just where does your staff draw the line? These pointers may help.

- **Doubles - to serve or not?** A double served with a mixer is more than twice as potent as a single shot diluted with a mixer because it means there'll be less mixer in the drink. Take this into account before offering too many incentives for your clientele to move up to doubles.

- **Discretion.** Many customers drink doubles at the same pace as they do singles, so more than a few drinking establishments have rules in place that ban the serving of doubles. The thinking behind this is decidedly mixed, with many bar operators preferring not to dictate to their customers what they can and cannot buy. You know your customers best, so use your best judgment.

- **Make sure your staff is firm and direct when refusing service to a customer.** If one bartender shows the slightest bit of leniency, a problem drinker will zero-in on that person and take advantage, now and in the future. If your people give in a little now, they may give in a little more tomorrow. Be firm!

- **Keep an eye on the people sitting with your "cut-off" customer.** Quite often they'll volunteer to get drinks for the person who is supposed to be cut off and if they do, your establishment is still liable for any injury.

- **Cut-off point.** Many experienced bartenders will talk to a customer before they get to the cut-off point and let them know that they're getting close to the line, before they get too drunk and belligerent. This is an especially important tip for dealing with younger people. They're generally less able to read their own level of drunkenness.

- **Excuses.** Sometimes a customer will attempt to get another drink by telling you that they live locally and are walking home. Regardless of the truth of this claim, it's still illegal to serve a visibly intoxicated customer, no matter what his or her situation. Simply explain the law to the customer and let him or her know that the bar could lose its license if servers are caught overserving customers.

- **Avoid embarrassment.** If you want to avoid embarrassing a good customer in front of others, simply ask to speak with them outside or away from listening ears. Explain the situation. A little consideration in this manner will mean a lot to a proud patron.

- **Nonalcoholic service.** When a customer is cut off from more alcohol, that doesn't mean they have to be cut off from service. Food, soda, coffee, iced tea - these are all great options to allow your tipsy customer a way to continue enjoying the evening without being sent home.

- **Other considerations.** Whenever you cut off a customer, make a small consideration to them in return. Offer to call them a cab, or even provide a free cup of coffee or bar snack. A small offering like this can only help you out of a tricky situation, not to mention leave you and your staff looking like good people.

CHAPTER SIX

THE LURE

Signature Drinks

Every great bar started as an empty bar. How do you get people in? How do you get them to come back? What motivation can you place in front of them to make them think of your place as their place? Many bars see the value in creating a special drink that becomes their signature creation. Such a lure can be a huge draw to your patrons, especially if it gives the customer great value, unique taste and an original bar experience. Successful specialty drinks invariably have an intriguing, captivating flavor not easily replicated without being privy to the recipe. If customers want to taste it again, they have to come back. These tips might provide you with just what you need:

- **Reputation.** A truly great signature drink can further the reputation of your bar. The drink, however, doesn't need to be particularly highbrow to become famous. For every huge establishment that creates an exotic fruit-rum-champagne concoction with a ten-dollar glass, there are five small neighborhood venues that can prepare one simple drink to perfection, for less money or in a unique way. A simple martini can be a signature creation if it's original-looking and tasty enough to get people talking.

- **Your signature drink should not be overpoweringly alcoholic.** Unless, of course, you want that to be its main draw! The idea should generally be for people to buy a lot of your signature drinks, not for them to buy one and stumble out the door into traffic.

- **Make your signature drink colorful or, at least, noticeably different.** A tiny squirt of Grenadine, Créme de Menthe or Blue Curacao can radically change the look of your signature drink without significantly altering the taste of it, at a low additional expense.

- **Garnishes don't have to be boring.** A slice of lemon or a wedge of celery might be traditional, but it's not exactly something your customers will get excited about. Try something out of left field - a stick of beef jerky, a wedge of kiwi, a chocolate Kit Kat or a Chupa Chup's lollipop. These might cost you a little more, but the novelty will leave a mark on your patrons.

- **Don't undermarket your creation.** Promote it like you would any other selling point of your bar, even to the extent of including it in your marketing material, e.g., "Welcome to Frankie's Bar: Home of the Flaming Deathbringer."

- **Make it special.** Your signature drink should be special on every level, including the glass in which it is served. A highball is not going to get across a message of excellence, so spend a little extra and put your drink in something that will add to the "ooh-aah" element.

- **Just giving a drink a fancy name won't make people buy them all night.** But giving them incredible value will. Your signature drink should be fairly (or even heavily) discounted, to add to the drawing power of the beverage for any non-regulars. Talk to your liquor distributor about whether they can cut you a deal to include one of their product lines in your creation so you can discount both the sale price and your cost.

- **Value.** Customers love to feel like they're getting great value for their money, and with a little tricky thinking, you can have your clientele believing they're being fed something with way more alcoholic than they actually are. For example, when pouring a tequila sunrise, if your bar server pours the orange juice and ice first, then drops the tequila in, the tequila will float to the bottom of the drink, ensuring that the customer's first sip from a straw will hit 'em like a brick. The drink will have no more alcohol than usual, and you shouldn't claim otherwise (that would be fraudulent), but it doesn't hurt for your patron to say to his or her friends, "Wow! They don't scrimp on the tequila in these things!"

- **Liquor on the glass rim.** Rubbing the inside rim of a glass with a liquor-soaked rim sponge will ensure that the first sip a customer takes will be the most memorable.

- **Hot cocoa, coffee and tea make a great base for signature drinks.** All have an attention-grabbing aroma and familiar flavor, and they combine nicely with lots of spirits and liqueurs - and they're very inexpensive!

- **Apple cider.** Consider hot apple cider as a signature drink base if your location is susceptible to cold weather. Cider marries well with many liqueurs to give a strong apple flavor to your patrons' favorite tastes.

Good Food, Happy Customers

The food you serve can sometimes be as profitable as, or even more profitable than, the drinks you sell. No matter what size your venue is, allowing your customers to go elsewhere to be fed is a cardinal sin - and a decent menu of bar snacks doesn't require a humongous kitchen.

- **Basics.** The number-one bar food staple is still the humble hamburger. With a small grill and some basic ingredients, you can offer your customers well over a dozen different varieties of burger. With the addition of a few other easy-to-prepare staples, such as nachos, sandwiches, chicken wings, fries, jack sticks and deep-fried mushrooms (not to forget the trusty salad), you can provide a wide array of bar food with only a grill, toaster oven and deep fryer.

- **Why stop at the good old predictable beef hamburger?** Turkey burgers, veggie burgers, chicken burgers, even teriyaki, tandoori and buffalo burgers, offer great variety to the burger connoisseur. Ingredients like Cajun spices, mozzarella, Gorgonzola, pepperoni, salsa and guacamole can add the kind of panache that will see people coming from far and wide to tuck one in.

- **Cook-your-own.** Some venues have gone a step further with their bar food and provide a "cook-your-own" facility, where customers can choose their ingredients, slap them on a large grill and cook their meat, cheese, vegetables, bun, etc., to their heart's content. While a setup such as this requires a certain level of investment and a high level of staff supervision, the returns can be outstanding.

- **To charcoal or not to charcoal?** Many operations feature a flame grill as a selling point for their bar food. But, many savvy chefs say that when cooking burgers, it's best to use a flat grill so that the juices don't run and the burger doesn't dry out. Along these lines, it's best not to put any weight on the burger when it's on the grill, as this, too, tends to dry out the meat.

- **Add a touch of originality to bar food.** Consider a touch of international flavor. A pasta bar containing a variety of pasta and sauce types that customers can mix and match is a very inexpensive alternative to standard bar snacks. Likewise, tempura, Chinese, curry and pizza can not only feed hungry mouths, but also attract a new stream of clientele looking for something that's a step up from burgers.

Exterior Tuning

How do your customers find you? Do they see ads in the local paper? Do their friends bring them? Chances are, neither of the two. Most customers will be people who have passed by and decided to try your venue. In order for this to happen, you need to pay far more attention to the exterior of your venue than most bar operators do. Here are some easy ways to spice up your outside areas:

- **A graphic projection lighting system.** Also known as a "bat light," this type of system can provide a greatly effective way to advertise your bar to passers-by. It also looks great when used on the inside of your establishment. Bat lights use a light and optic setup to project your logo or other related graphics onto any surface, including walls, ceilings, the outside sidewalk and more. They can be purchased or hired for far less than you might think. Talk to High End Systems (www.highend.com, 512-836-2242) about their Technobeam system to see if your budget can handle a little high-tech marketing.

- **How far down the road can your bar be seen?** If you can't be seen for at least a block away, consider increasing your outside signage. While this is not a small expense, there's no point in hiding the fact that your bar is nearby. If you talk to your distributors, you might find that one of them is prepared to subsidize the cost of your signage in return for mention of their product. Soda companies do this for convenience stores all the time.

- **Neon works!** Why do you think every bar has neon beer signs in the window? The answer is simple: because people notice them, and they don't cost a lot to produce. An impressive neon sign is a local landmark - think of those huge neon signs in Times Square and how many tourists know of them and send photos of them home to the family. You don't have to go to quite that scale, but a small investment in neon will bring people in to take a closer look.

- **Don't discount the appeal of a nice paint job.** Is your exterior freshly painted? Is it boring old white? Wouldn't a lick of paint transform things? A new paint job isn't just about aesthetics; the outside of your venue is usually presumed to reflect the inside. Consider asking your staff to come in after-hours and paint the walls for you in return for a bonus payment. Most bar staff could use a few hundred bucks extra now and then. It'll be a lot cheaper than hiring professionals.

- **Landscaping isn't a luxury.** Just as your exterior walls say a lot about your interior, so, too do your grounds. If all you have outside your venue is a gravel-covered parking lot and a few beat-up pickup trucks, you're not exactly going to attract a broad demographic, no matter what you offer inside. Plant some hardy plants outside that will brave weather extremes and not need constant trimming and watering. They will soften the outside of your bar exterior. A few trees around the outside of the parking lot won't hurt, and some up-lights underneath them can offer a particularly breathtaking look for a reasonable price.

Human Entertainment Doesn't Stop at Live Bands

Many bar operators like to keep their patrons entertained by a variety of eclectic means and don't mind spending a few dollars to do so. In fact, major sporting venues have been employing these kinds of "half time" entertainments for years and finding great results. Consider the following:

- **Trivia nights.** A handful of questions, a few slips of paper for answers, a running score and $50 worth of vouchers for food and drink to give away - it all makes for a big night of entertainment. More and more venues are seeing the value of trivia competitions; luring customers in with the offer of freebies. These contests vary from huge nights run by live presenters to computerized interactive trivia games, where patrons compete against patrons in other bars around the country via satellite. Either option does one important thing: bring people back.

- **Live psychic readings.** A live psychic on a given night of the week doing palm readings, tarot card readings and horoscopes can bring in a dedicated brand of believers on a regular basis. Offering a psychic $100 a night to look after your customers' needs is a simple option, and if she's any good, your patrons will not only line up for more, but they'll also cross her palm with plenty of tips.

- **Massages.** Who doesn't like their shoulders rubbed by a professional masseuse or masseur? Offering your patrons free massages on a given night is a guaranteed way to get new blood in the door. It also gives your old blood a little pick-me-up. If your patrons know they'll get a massage by coming in on a Monday night, you can bet they'll be there every single Monday.

- **Karaoke.** The Japanese tradition of karaoke has come on in leaps and bounds in North America in the last ten years, but there's still a big difference between quality karaoke and most karaoke. It's far more than simply putting up a bunch of old Neil Diamond songs with some fuzzy video. Your karaoke enthusiasts need variety in the music selection. Hire a good karaoke host who can keep things moving and, most important, draw a big crowd of listeners. Give the people what they need.

- **Board games.** A Scrabble or Monopoly night might be a really simple idea, but it works! Quieter nights of the week are an excellent time to try out a board game tournament. It instills a sense of community amongst your patrons. When a new customer has to play against two regulars and another newbie for two hours, chances are that by the end you'll have a table of four regulars on your hands.

- **Stand-up comedy.** They don't cost a fortune to put on. Most stand-up comedians are happy just to get an audience and a few bucks' gas money, and though quality certainly costs, it's more than possible for you to find four or five stand-up comedians who will keep your audience laughing without costing you more than a hundred bucks total. Live comedy is a great draw and it tends to keep an audience planted until the finish. Try an open mike night and see what you find!

Can Discounts Do You More Damage than Good?

In a survey taken by Nightclub and Bar Magazine and NTN Entertainment, a cross-section of bar patrons were asked what would be most likely to get them to try a new bar. Of the respondents, 45 percent said food and drink discounts would be their prime motivator, while only 22 percent said special events would grab their attention. Somewhat interesting: 11 percent suggested that Internet access would get them to try somewhere new. But while most venues offer discounts as their big lure for new customers, can that hurt more than your bottom line?

- **Discounts.** Needless to say, discounts reduce your profit margin. Generally, they won't increase what a person spends in a night, only what you give them for the same money.

- **Offering lower prices can be perceived as a bargain.** Unfortunately, it can also change perceptions on the worth of your bar. A big sign out front that trumpets dollar beers will attract certain people for sure. However, are they really the people you want?

- **One night per week?** A discount on one night trains your customers to come only on that night. In fact, when they're used to paying that discount, the "normal price" nights may even seem expensive to them: "Why pay three bucks on a Sunday when it costs only one on a Monday?"

- **Discounts don't attract loyal customers.** They'll see past a discount and appreciate the other qualities your venue boasts. What discounts attract are one-off customers, walk-by and drive-by traffic and, for the most part, cheapskates. Relying purely on the discount as a means of converting one of these patrons to "regular" status is a no-win situation. You have to show customers that there are other reasons for frequenting your establishment.

- **Despite the above, a discount is not something to be avoided.** However, it should be used judiciously. Offer a variety of good deals that don't rely on discounts, such as special events, giveaways, games, entertainment, good food and Internet access. Unlike discounts, these sorts of promotions add value to your perceived image rather than detract from it.

Good Marketing Is Essential

Discounts and freebies to bring in new customers are all well and good, but doesn't it make more sense to market to a larger segment of people? Spending a little can bring you a lot, if you're bringing in the right kind of people and enough of them. Consider the following:

- **Open bar.** Offer local companies an open bar for an hour and/or a free buffet if they bring more than 25 people on a Friday night after work. Sure, initially you'll lose money on the deal, but if your venue is well run, fun and offers good value for their money, they'll stay on well past the free hour. Your venue could potentially become the company's new after-hours haunt.

- **TGIF promotion.** For example, anyone wearing a tie receives a big drink discount on a Friday afternoon. Workplace get-togethers are a great source of large groups. If you can make your venue a regular weekly stop, those people will begin to bring friends and partners on other nights of the week, too.

- **Large industry groups.** Emergency workers, for example, often hold evenings for those in that industry to get together and let their hair down. Contact local unions, Chambers of Commerce and any other representative body in your area. See if they'd be interested in hosting an event at your venue. If they need convincing, offer a discount on food and drink, or suggest possibilities such as free DJ entertainment, for the night. Every time you bring in one of these groups, you're showing your wares to hundreds of people who may otherwise never have set foot in your venue.

- **Contact a local radio station.** Suggest they run a live broadcast from your venue on a regular basis. This kind of publicity helps them (They'd love to drink free and would probably ask for a little advertising from you), and it certainly helps you to be seen as such a great venue that the local radio station wants to hang out there.

Treat Your Customers Like VIPs

Many venues find that supplying VIP cards to patrons is a great way to bring one-off customers back for more, without spending a whole lot of money. These small, business-card-sized membership cards can be bought in large numbers relatively inexpensively. If you opt for a magnetic strip system, you can even keep track of whom your best customers are.

- **Parties and functions.** When you have a function or party at your venue, make a point of giving all the guests a VIP card registration form. On this they'll put their name, address, birthdate and e-mail address, which you should keep in a database. At a later date, send these people a letter telling them their card is ready to be picked up - they'll visit you again, and you'll be one step closer to turning them into regular customers.

- **Mailing list.** VIP card data can be invaluable and will help you in many areas. Use it to send out a quarterly mailing inviting those on your list to partake in a special offer. Update them on what's going on at your venue this month, etc.

- **Birthdays.** Send a special mailing out to everyone having a birthday each month. Offer your venue as the location for their birthday parties, with drink discounts and a DJ if they bring 25 people or more. If there's no charge for the party holders, they'll gladly accept your offer, and when the party is underway, offer their guests VIP card applications and start the process all over again.

Every seat is full, and potential customers, unwilling to wait, are walking out the door in droves. It hurts every time it happens. But what can you do about it? If the tables aren't ready, the tables just aren't ready, right? Wrong! You can't fit people into tables that don't exist, but you can give your customers a reason (or five) to wait around. In fact, integrating the wait into the entire experience of being in your establishment can not only prevent walkouts, it can extend your peak periods significantly.

- **Parking lot problems.** The first place you're likely to lose customers on a busy night is in your parking lot. If there's a line outside the door, all it takes is a little creativity to either bring the line inside or disguise it on the outside. Remember, those people waiting outside are real thirsty, and they'd be more than happy to do their waiting in a courtyard area, at a temporary bar, or in a cordoned-off outside area where drinking is permitted.

- **Beyond the line.** Of those who are prepared to brave the "line," most will do so gladly if they know they can be inside within 30 minutes. Also, it's simple to change waiting time perceptions by making that wait a little more comfortable, entertaining or busy.

- **Parking can be a big hassle in many venues.** If there tends to be a logjam outside your venue, consider installing a valet service on busy nights or posting a staff member outside to direct patrons to parking around the back or down the road. Clear signs pointing to parking areas also help.

- **Employ a stand-up comedian to "work" the outside crowd.** TV shows do this to get an audience warmed up before the taping of a TV show. There's no reason it can't be of benefit to warm up your crowd while they wait.

- **Think about your TV screens and sound system in relation to your waiting area.** Can waiting people catch a glimpse of the big game? Can they hear the music inside? These things will keep a waiting person keen on staying around, whereas a blank brick wall and a disinterested bouncer isn't inviting to anyone.

- **Keep clientele informed.** If there's a wait for a table, set up an electronic sign indicating how long their expected wait will be. Add to this anything you can think of that will make their wait more entertaining; sports scores, trivia questions, coming events. It might be a little more work, but if you can keep just five people from leaving, it'll be worth it. Contact Daktronics (www.daktronics.com) by calling 605-697-4000.

- **What's wrong with giving away a freebie or ten?** Offer your waiting patrons a little something extra and they won't just tolerate waiting, they'll do so gladly. Coupons to be used on a later date are a good option.

- **It doesn't have to be expensive.** Giving your waiting customers something to do doesn't have to be expensive, high-tech or take up your employees' valuable time. Consider offering free reading material or even Internet access in your waiting area.

- **Act first.** A long wait doesn't seem quite so long when a staff member keeps you informed on how long your table will take. Don't wait for the customers to ask you; just go out and tell them.

The Internet Can Help You

Does your bar have a web site? If no, why not? An Internet home for your establishment doesn't have to cost the earth. If you incorporate a little smart thinking into the mix, you can turn the World Wide Web into a unique marketing tool and, also, an attraction for those who might not otherwise have made the trip into your venue.

- **Create a web site for your bar** - not just a quickie page with a logo, your phone number and business hours, but a real, working web site - something that make people come back again and again. Check out the web site for the Hooters chain (www.hooters.com). This franchise not only provides information on their bar/ restaurant locations, but their Web site also incorporates humor, pictures, the history of their company and even calendars of their waitresses and Hooters merchandise. The House of Blues does likewise (www.houseofblues.com). This kind of brand building not only brings in more customers, but it can also bring an additional revenue stream through merchandise sales.

Need a web site? Contact Gizmo Graphics Web design; they offer low-cost, high-quality Web design services, hosting services and Web maintenance services catering to the food service industry and individual small businesses (www.gizwebs.com).

- **Incorporate your customers into your web site.** Invest in a digital camera or two and take pictures of your patrons on busy nights. It's then a relatively simple task to transfer those pictures to your web site. Your customers will not only check for themselves, they will also point out the site to their friends. A live web-cam is also a good promotional tool, allowing people to check on the crowd from home before they even leave the house.

- **Live-streaming.** Investigate what it would take to feature live band performances on your web site. Live-streaming sound and video isn't an inexpensive option for your bar and the bands might ask to be compensated for allowing you to pipe their performance over the Internet. However, offering this service to your customers when they can't make it to your bar can only grow your reputation and make your venue a regular online - as well as off-line - stop.

- **Incorporate Internet access into the services your bar provides its customers.** Setting up a few Internet terminals is not an incredibly expensive task, and it will bring in customers looking for quick net access - with the accompanying drink and food that this business will provide. Whether you offer free net access or decide to recoup some costs by charging a per-hour rate, this expense will be quickly returned in increased business. For information on Internet kiosks, contact KIS at 303-466-5471 (www.kis-kiosk.com).

- **Quiet space.** More and more, customers are looking for a quiet place to work, read or study; sit with a laptop computer in places like cafés, bars and restaurants. In response to this trend, many public facilities, such as airports, hotels, cafés, libraries and bars, are outfitting their establishments with power outlets nearby all seating areas so that customers can 'plug in' and stay all day. To further this, some savvy business owners are even supplying phone outlets, so that their laptop-wielding patrons can get online - further extending the length of their stay.

CHAPTER SEVEN

THE PROFITS

What Does Each Drink Cost You?

Without profits, you're out of business, but so many managers see profits as what the owners worry about. Your job is as much to grow profits as to sustain them, so consider putting a little elbow grease into the growth of your establishment by learning about the nickel and dime stuff. A good bar operator needs to wear a number of hats, but the four most important are that of promoter, psychologist, host and accountant. This isn't to say that you need to be of professional standard in all four areas, but you do need a working knowledge of each area, so that you can fine-tune those aspects of your business. On the accounting side of things, you need to be able to assess what every piece of your business costs. Also, as your spirits and liqueurs are a very large segment of your inventory, you should learn exactly how much each and every drink you sell actually costs you. Follow these exercises and you'll be able to assess exactly which drinks bring you the highest profit margin and which drinks could use a price increase.

- **Cost per ounce.** There is 33.8 ounces in a liter, so if you're paying $15 a liter for a certain spirit, simply dividing that amount by 33.8 will bring you the beverage's ounce cost (in this case, $0.44). If your bottle size is 750ml, then divide the bottle cost by 25.35 to get the ounce cost. Likewise, dividing a 500ml bottle by 16.9 will give you that product's ounce cost.

- **Total beverage cost.** When calculating what it costs you to provide a mixed drink to a customer, simply figure out the ounce cost of each item in the drink. A half-shot means adding half the ounce cost of that shot, whereas a double shot would mean doubling the ounce cost. Make sure to include every aspect of the drink, such as mixers, dashes of cordial and garnishes. The total of each of these ounce costs will be your "beverage cost" for that drink.

- **Cost percentage.** When you're investing in inventory, you want to know that you're getting a good return on your money and the best way to figure out your percentage return is to estimate your cost percentage for each drink you sell. Simply divide your ounce cost (or bottle cost) by the sale price you've set for that item and then multiply that number by 100. The total will tell you exactly what percentage of the final drink price you are spending on the purchase of its raw contents. The lower the number, the more profit you're making.

- **Gross profit margin.** To figure out each item's gross profit, simply deduct the cost price from the sale price. To figure out your gross profit margin, take the gross profit, divide it by the sales price and multiply it by 100. The figure remaining is your gross profit margin. You may well find it varies greatly from beverage to beverage. This will tell you which items have a high enough profit margin to push on your customers and which items are just making up the numbers.

Protecting Your Profits

Your profit margin, like that of any business, is fragile at best. You can sit down with a calculator and try to calculate the exact percentage you'd like to see on each drink. But in practice, a little splash too much here and there can see you falling perilously close to a loss. Follow these rules and you'll be that much more likely to see your bottom line behind the bar match that of your balance sheet estimations.

- **Watch what your staff pours.** Regularly measure what they consider an ounce. If just one bartender overpours 40 shots a night by 25 percent, you've given away ten drinks for nothing. This kind of waste can get very expensive, especially if you have a large bar staff and they're all pouring more than 40 drinks per night.

- **Have your staff keep all the liquor in the glass.** Many staff members get lazy as the night wears on, and inevitably they'll start taking shortcuts. One shortcut many take is to line up three or four glasses and pour one after the other in a straight line without raising the head of the bottle. While this may save them a second or two, it also pours a lot of your product directly onto the bar surface, not to mention down the sides of the glasses that your customers are about to put in their hands. It also means your customers are far less likely to get what they've paid for. Don't let it happen.

- **There are alternatives to free-pouring.** While free-pouring certainly is more stylish and perhaps faster than measured pouring, it is also definitely far from accurate. As bar staff generally tend to err on the side of caution, they usually pour too much rather than too little. Control-pour spouts, such as our or Posi-Pour spouts, are a little more expensive than the usual free-pour systems, but they give a far more accurate pour without the need for clunky overhead systems or sophisticated electronics - and at much the same speed as free-pourers. Take a look at Posi-Pour portion-control pour spouts at www.atlantic-pub.com.

- **Liquor control system.** If you really want to keep an eye on your outgoings, a liquor control system may be your answer. These computer-controlled systems feature an attachment on the neck of the bottle that measures how much liquid is being dispensed, without stopping the flow after every ounce, like the control-pour spouts do. These systems can be linked to your computer system so that you can get accurate usage stats on your desktop, but the price of setting these systems up can be prohibitive. Then again, you get what you pay for. Contact TruMeasur at www.trumeasur.com.

- **Are computer-controlled systems as acceptable to customers as free-pour setups?** The simple answer - though many guess it to be no - is yes. In a study published in the Journal of Hospitality and Leisure Marketing in 1999, Professor Carl Borchgrevink, Ph.D., CFBE of the Michigan State School of Hospitality Business, concluded that bar customers being served from computer-controlled systems on one night and handheld jiggers the next noticed a negligible amount of difference between the two, especially if the computer-controlled system clearly showed the brand being poured and the amount being dispensed. The lesson here is not to fear technology.

Structuring a Price List

Guesswork just won't do in today's corporate world. Figuring that, if your scotch costs you $14 a bottle, you can sell a shot for $3 is just a little hit-and-miss when you take in all the other potential costs, like rent, insurance and wages, that your establishment has to cover over the course of a month. It's possible you might be able to charge less than $3, but it's also possible you should be charging way more. Take these factors into account when making your next price list adjustment:

- **Market positioning.** Take a look around at what your competitors are charging. Figure out if you need to undercut them or match their level. Does your establishment give added value enough to increase your prices and still draw a good crowd? Are you a level above them in terms of services and product? Are you evenly matched? Are you looking for a more "low rent" crowd? Price accordingly.
- **The competition.** They're not always right, but

if they've been around a while, your direct competitors probably have a good gauge of what your local customers are prepared to pay for a drink. Take the time to look around and take particular note of any specials they offer on certain nights.

- **Customer demographics.** Are your patrons blue-collar workers? Are they white-collar? Do they have families to get home to or are they likely to stay all night and spend every penny? Are they young adults or senior citizens? These all impact what you can charge without losing clientele, and you should have the information already from your market research.

- **Embrace simplicity.** It's far better for your customers and staff to have to deal with a simple pricing structure as opposed to forcing them to break their brains over an intricate maze of differently priced products. Set across-the-board levels of prices; for example, well spirits might cost $3, middle-shelf $3.50 and top-shelf $4. Of course there's always going to be the occasional variation, but for the most part, a three-tiered system gives you flexibility in pricing without your staff continually needing to check a price list or hand out handfuls of change.

- **Include tax in your pricing.** There's nothing worse than getting $0.84 change from a five-dollar bill on every drink you buy and getting home with a pocket full of silver and copper. If you're going to set your prices at a round level, include the tax in that price so you can use price levels to your advantage. If your alcohol tax rate is 10 percent, the non-tax price for a shot that costs your patrons $3.50 would be $3.18 ($3.18 plus tax of $0.32 equals $3.49). Let your accountant do the math, not your bar staff. Sales tax is a complicated matter that varies dramatically from state to state. Prior to establishing the net price inclusive of tax, discuss the issue with your accountant and state Department of Revenue. Don't find out later in a five-year audit that you've been calculating the tax incorrectly.

Up-sizing Is Essential

When you go to the movies, quite often you can buy a double-sized popcorn for only $0.75 more than the $3.50 regular size. This would seem to be an astonishing bonus for the customer, so why does the cinema operator push this "up-sizing" so hard? Quite simply, because they're selling about $0.04 worth of popcorn for that extra $0.75. That second portion might not bring as large a profit margin as the first, but it's still profit. Your drinks run the same way - if you can get another buck out of a customer selling a drink that costs you $0.45 to prepare, it's worth doing.

- **Consider the cost per ounce of your well spirits.** Let's assume you're using El Cheapo brand tequila at a base cost of $7.54 a liter. That would mean that an ounce of that spirit is costing your establishment $0.22, while a more-expensive brand of tequila, let's say Cuervo for the sake of this example, might come at a base cost of $14 per liter, or $0.41 per shot. Common thinking might lead you to say that by using the cheaper tequila you're saving yourself $0.19 on every drink sold. But, if you consider the alternative of up-selling the more expensive spirit for an extra $0.80 or so, you're actually making an extra $0.61 profit on every up-sized drink.

- **Offer your customers a discount to spend more than they planned.** This works in other areas, too. Turning a single into a double for an additional dollar, or selling half-price burgers with every shot of a specific brand of spirit, brings you more money per order, while bringing your customers added value. Your profit margin might not be as high, but you'll be extracting more money from your customers than they might otherwise have spent - a definite win-win.

- **Up-selling.** Most bar customers will bring out more money than they initially want to spend - just in case - especially those that don't have easy access to it through ATM machines and credit cards, so it's imperative that your staff don't let those customers walk out the door having spent less than they planned. Incentives for up-selling are commonplace in the theater and fast-food industries, so why not offer your staff an incentive to up-sell and watch your better staff earn a few extra dollars while earning you hundreds?

- **Incentives.** For example, if a member of your staff engages someone in conversation and discovers they're looking for somewhere to hold a private function, birthday party, girls' night out -

any large gathering of people - there's certainly no harm in making it worth their while to bring that prospective client to you. Twenty dollars here, $50 there - even a percentage of the bar take - if you offer the incentives, you'll be surprised how far people will go to bring you new business.

Extracting More from Every Customer

The patron walks in with $20. When the well is dry, he or she will go home (or possibly procure more) but how do you make sure you get as much of that $20 as possible? Consider the following:

- **Value-add!** It might cost you a buck to make a bourbon and coke and it might cost you two bucks to make a burger. Why not offer your drinkers a cut-price deal on that burger during a certain time of the night: buy two drinks, get a free burger to go with it. You're not making any money on that burger, but you are ensuring that the customer will stay in your bar while they eat it - and probably a little longer. Heck, they might even order a side of deep-fried mushrooms to go along with it.

- **Make it easier to stay than go.** If your staff is asking people, "Should I get you the bill?" instead of, "How about a round of coffees?" you're only giving your customers an excuse to hit the road.

- **Keep the TV interesting.** A big error many establishments make is that they leave a TV on but don't pay any attention to what's on it. Keep an eye on your screens and keep an even bigger eye on the TV Guide, to make sure that, if at all possible, you're giving your patrons a reason to stay: "Ooh, ER is on! Maybe I'll have another..."

- **Read the crowd.** On any given night, your entire customer base can change radically. If you look around and find that there are a lot of young people in the place, adapt to suit that audience. Run a one-off special on tequila shots or shooters or turn on the dance-floor lights. Likewise, if a sports crowd comes in unexpectedly, get them into the swing of things by adapting to suit their needs.

- **Give valued employees the power to make executive decisions**. There's nothing worse, as a customer, than being told, "I don't know, the manager isn't here until later tonight..." Make sure you always have people on staff who can handle a situation and even veer away from the way things normally run, if common sense dictates it. Trust your people to make the right move.

- **Cut down on your "no" answers.** You might stock Diet Coke, but what about Diet 7-Up? What about veggie burgers? What about fresh-squeezed orange juice? There might not be a whole lot of demand for these products, but if you don't have them when they're asked for, you're giving your customers an excuse not to return, even if they don't make a big deal about it at the time. Don't sink money into something that won't sell, but don't go the other way and reduce what you can sell.

- **Merchandise sells!** A funky logo doesn't just make your venue more appealing; it sells, too. Research shows that the McDonald's logo is more recognizable to children than the cross symbol of Christianity; so it stands to reason that you could profit nicely from a logo that is "cool" enough for people to wear. T-shirts, golf shirts, baseball caps, key chains, lighters and souvenir glasses - take a tip from the Hard Rock Café: if sold well, merchandise can be a bigger earner than alcohol.

Vending Machines Pay

Your kitchen can't stay open all night long and when it closes, it will do you well to have a means for your customers to fill a hole in their stomachs. A vending machine will not only do just that, it can also supply everything from condoms to cologne, antacids to breath mints. In fact, if there's a need for it, you can bet there's a vending machine to fill that need. Check your local yellow pages for vending suppliers near you.

- **Respond to customer requirements.** People go to bars for three reasons: to drink, have fun and meet people. That last reason might make you want to consider fitting your club with a condom machine. One of these machines in the women's and men's restrooms can bring you a great source of income, especially on busy nights. Offering other bathroom essentials, like cologne, lip balm, women's essentials and aspirin, can add further profitability to your operation.

- **Snacks.** A selection of snack products can be another great earner, not just inside your bar but also outside. Chocolates, candy, chips, mints, cookies, granola bars; these snacks will keep your patrons going all night long without bothering your bar staff - or tempting them to enjoy the snacks themselves. Also, if you have some machines positioned outside your venue, they will continue selling for you even when the bar is closed!

- **Water.** In a nightclub, charging for glasses of water can be seen as profiteering by your customers. However, installing a bottled-water-vending machine can not only save your bartenders the time spent pouring out free water, it can also bring you in a hefty profit when patrons start to work up a sweat on the dance floor. Initiate a "bottled water only" rule when the dance floor is in operation and have your bartenders point to the vending machine whenever they're asked for water. Or have a selection of bottled waters available from the bar. You might even consider a special menu just for bottled waters. Your customers won't mind paying for it so much if they're getting the bottled product.

- **Pay phones.** It seems everyone these days has a cell phone, but there's still a huge need for the good old payphone. Incorporating phone card vending machines alongside a bank of pay phones is a way to double your profits on your customers' phone habits. Have them give you quarters for local calls or ten bucks for long distance. If you give your patrons options, they'll invariably choose one.

The Business Plan

Certainly a having business plan is important before opening the doors of any new business, and it's imperative if you decide to expand what you have. However, there are many pitfalls to avoid:

- **Make it workable.** A business plan is useless unless the person writing it is A) the person who will start the business, and B) understands the marketplace personally. Investors will frown upon a business plan composed by someone other than the proposed management. Using outsiders, such as a business plan writer or consulting service, is fine, but if they're putting the entire plan together, why does an investor need you?

- **Do you really need a business plan before you have investment in place?** Most of the time, all you really need is a simple executive summary, which is an 8- to-10 page synopsis of your plan, rather than a 50-page business plan. Most investors have no interest in wading through a massive document filled with complex (and largely unsubstantiated) business projections.

- **Online resources.** When you do need a business

plan, there are numerous online resources that can walk you through the process so that your mark is on every page and the end result is just what you need. Take a look at Quickplan™ at www.atlantic-pub.com.

- **Projections.** Many business-plan books will tell you that you need to make cash-flow projections for up to six years. But in the bar business, which has variables, that can change completely every few years; such projections are nigh impossible to make. Don't make a fool of yourself, trying show off with fancy numbers that can't be substantiated.

- **Business plan outline.** If you decide to create a comprehensive business plan, be sure to include all pertinent information. The chart on the next page outlines what needs to be included.

Business Plan Outline

I.   **Cover sheet**
II. **Statement of purpose**
III. **Table of contents**
IV. **The Business**
   A. Description of business
   B. Marketing
   C. Competition
   D. Operating procedures
   E. Personnel
   F. Business insurance
   G. Financial data
V.   **Financial Data**
   A. Loan applications
   B. Capital equipment and supply list
   C. Balance sheet
   D. Breakeven analysis
   E. Pro-forma income projections (profit and loss statements)
      1. Three-year summary
      2. Detail by month, first year
      3. Detail by quarters, second and third years
      4. Assumptions upon which projections were based
   F. Pro-forma cash flow
      1. Follow guidelines for number 5.
VI. **Supporting Documents**
   A. Tax returns of principals for last three years
   B. Personal financial statement (all banks have these forms)
   C. In the case of a franchised business, a copy of franchise contract and all supporting documents provided by the franchisor
   D. Copy of proposed lease or purchase agreement for building space
   E. Copy of licenses and other legal documents
   F. Copy of resumes of all principals
   G. Copies of letters of intent from suppliers, etc.

The nightclub industry is unlike any other.

CHAPTER EIGHT

THE EXPANSION

Starting a Nightclub

So your bar has turned a good profit and you're on the way to capturing more of the market. What next? Ever considered a nightclub? The nightclub industry is unlike any other, and when you have a popular bar and restaurant operation, many people will approach you with grand plans to expand into the club business, while portraying themselves as skilled experts in the nightclub field. While some indeed do know what they're talking about, nightclubs have an incredibly high rate of failure; in fact, approximately 10 percent of the nightclubs out there make 80 percent of nightclub revenue. Don't just take anyone's word on opening a nightclub - know what you're doing going in.

- **First thing first.** You must have the ability to understand people on a leisure level. Most successful people in the club game have experienced every position a nightclub has to offer, from glass collector to manager. They know exactly how the nightclub entertainment marketplace is driven. If you've never worked in a nightclub before, go get a job in one for a month before spending your hard-earned money on one of your own.

- **Read up on the nightclub business before you spend a cent.** There are plenty of resources, both online and off-line, that can give you in-depth information on the do's and don'ts of opening a nightclub.

- **Check out the competition.** Spend a night in as many local clubs as you can - both successful ones and unsuccessful ones. Take notes on who is doing what, what seems to hit a chord with the locals and what might work, for a relatively small investment, with your own establishment.

- **Develop you own niche.** You'll rarely take the industry by storm, but if you find a decent-sized sector of the market that is underserved and manage to fill that need well, you'll go a long way towards turning in a healthy and consistent profit.

DJ or Computer?

Sometimes the size of a bar operation doesn't warrant an investment in a DJ, but that doesn't mean that the music selection can't be fashioned to suit a crowd, nor does it mean that the establishment can't boast itself as a venue to come and dance.

- **MP3 mixer.** A computer system with a wide selection of MP3s and an auto mixing program like MP3000f can keep the tunes rolling all night with the sort of seamless, nonstop sound that you'd normally get from a DJ. Though an MP3 mixer isn't capable of following the crowd's mood, it's a cost-effective means of putting together a DJ sound without spending a fortune. MP3000f can be downloaded at www.disconova.com.

- **Find a good DJ.** Though an auto mixing system is a very cost-effective option, if you really want to keep a crowd at maximum pleasure level, a good DJ is a must. However, finding a good, reliable DJ who loosens up the crowd is often difficult. Run a competition for local hopefuls and offer the winner a regular gig with you.

- **Own equipment.** Many DJs have their own sound equipment, lighting and music, but they also charge a far higher price as a result. Purchase your own sound equipment and lighting. Pay a DJ by the hour; it's far more cost effective in the long-term. It also allows you to hire DJs without their own equipment, thus expanding your hiring possibilities.

- **Please the crowd.** Many DJs play music for their own pleasure rather than the crowd's, and as a result, the dance floor can become a little quiet sometimes. To ensure your DJ not only works the crowd well, but also brings people back every week, offer him or her a small percentage of the register take for the night. This consideration will not only have your DJ trying harder to keep the patrons there all night, but will also ensure he or she doesn't move on to a new job at the drop of a hat - something many DJs are prone to do.

- **VideoCD and DVD.** Gone are the days when a quality establishment could get away with relying on a CD player behind the bar or a jukebox to keep the customers' ears entertained. VideoCD and DVD are now taking over. Download music, video, even karaoke, for free off the Internet. If you create enough variety in these DVDs, your bar staff can conceivably throw on a disc and forget it for hours, while your customers dance to, sing along with and even watch their favorite music. Please note that establishments that play live or recorded music must be licensed with BMI and ASCAP. You can find them online at www.bmi.com/home.asp and www.ascap.com.

- **Auto changers.** If you elect to use a VideoCD system, auto changers can be used to enable DJs or bar staff to mix up the programming without any manual tweaking over the course of the night. Tracks can be simply programmed by the user or randomly selected by the player. VideoCD not only covers all of the popular music mediums, but it also can be customized and mixed - an option that DVD doesn't yet match.

Creating a Dance Floor

Just about any bar establishment can benefit from an area set aside for dancing, even if only for a few nights of the week. But, what's the best way to go about creating one?

- **Square footage.** Most bar operators find that setting aside anywhere between 10 percent and 15 percent of the venue's total square footage for a dance floor is a winning formula. A dance floor should be large enough to hold a good number of people, but if it is too large it often can feel empty and exposed. Many people who dance like the privacy a crowd offers them, so making your dance floor too large can detract from their enjoyment.

- **Dedicated dance floor?** A dance floor doesn't have to be dedicated to one use. At times of the week when dancing isn't taking place, it can be turned into a stage area for live entertainment, or even removed altogether if you invest in a portable dance floor. Portable dance floor systems may be found at www.tuffdeck.com and www.dance-2000.com.

- **Slippery surfaces.** While a well-polished dance floor can be great for dancers, it can be a slipping hazard for your customers - especially if they've had a little to drink. To avoid costly injury claims, ensure your staff always place adequate warning signs on a dance floor when it is not being used for that purpose.

Sound Systems

Whether or not you're featuring live entertainment or a fully functioning dance floor, a strong and flexible sound system is an integral part of your bar operation. Consider the following:

- **Don't underestimate your needs.** When it comes to constructing a quality sound system, it's far better to overdo your capacity and cut back as you need to, than to strain amps and fatigue speakers prematurely.

- **Loud music can be great if the crowd has come seeking it.** Or, indeed, if a dance floor is an integral part of your business. But it also interferes with the very interaction that your patrons have come to enjoy. If you can't set aside a quieter area for your customers to use when talking, consider lowering the volume of your music. This won't just make your customers more relaxed; it will also make the process of ordering a drink easier.

- **Consider the acoustics of your venue when setting up your sound system.** If the bar or seating area faces a dance floor or live entertainment stage, having your speaker system aimed towards the bar will only make service and interaction difficult during loud music periods. Consider positioning your speakers between the dance floor/stage and bar areas. Point them away from the areas of your venue that will benefit from being quieter.

- **Video walls.** Pair these popular enhancements with a quality sound system. A video wall can produce an awesome effect that, while not adding to the sound, can certainly improve how the patrons perceive it. A 16-cube video wall isn't only a dance floor supplement; it can also be great for daytime coverage of sporting events and is also useful for presentations during corporate functions. Contact Multivision Video and Film at www.vidwall.com.

Coins In - Customers Happy

Coin-operated entertainment machines are a great source of extra revenue for a bar. The eclectic nature of most bars means that coin-ops of all styles, sizes and functions can fit perfectly within your surroundings while adding to the fun and flavor of your establishment. The profits that coin-ops generate can be huge; they can also run a lot deeper than just the money inserted into the machines. Coin-ops increase traffic, generate great repeat business and keep people in your venue far longer. From high-tech games to virtual reality to pool tables, anything that gives your customers added entertainment is a good option - especially if it will bring you higher profits.

- **Profit based coin-ops.** Some coin-ops don't have to cost you a cent, but they can bring in a good source of revenue. Simply look in the yellow pages under "coin-operated" and you'll find a slew of companies who will bring you games and entertainment for your customers for absolutely no charge - other than a share of the profits. This kind of a deal can only be good for your business. No maintenance worries, and you

125

get a new machine whenever an old one stops earning money - all free of charge.

- **Deal directly with the machine manufacturers.** In a situation like this, your venue will handle most of the daily maintenance required on the machines, and the manufacturer's repairmen will come out only as needed. Although initially this limits your selection of game alternatives, when you do want to switch games, it's only a matter of changing a couple of computer chips. The actual game casing stays the same, but with a switch of the motherboard, a completely different game appears, keeping your customers from getting bored with your options.

- **Responsibility.** Don't fall into the trap with coin-ops where your employees don't want to know when they're malfunctioning. If the machine is on your premises, take responsibility for it and either return the customer's money or see to it that someone on staff can open and correct the machine in question. Similarly, ensure that your supplier can fix a malfunctioning machine ASAP, there's nothing worse than someone coming in to play a machine and finding it switched off - again.

- **One of the biggest crazes at the moment is photo machines.** Customers put up to five dollars into the machine and step in to have their photos taken. In a few minutes they can have their image on stickers or postcards - they can even pick a background. Or, if they want to get really extravagant, they can have their partner get their photo taken and have the machine create an image of what their child would look like. These machines are huge moneymakers and can even incorporate an ad for your bar within the picture. Your local yellow pages will list plenty of suppliers.

- **Dancing machines.** These are extremely popular. Patrons throw a dollar into the machine and step up onto a stage that features a series of lights. They then try to step on whichever lights flash to keep in time with an on-screen dancer. These sorts of machines can be very addictive and often draw a large crowd - which can't hurt your bar takings. Again, any amusement machine vendor in your local yellow pages should be able to supply this machine to you.

- **Virtual reality sports are becoming a reality.** More and more bars are installing VR golf ranges, VR batting cages, VR racing games, VR bowling alleys, VR hockey games and VR boxing machines that allow customers to "virtually" beat the heck out of each other. These machines are the same as any other coin-operated gaming machine, except that they cost the customer more and deliver a superior product. While they take up a little more room, they give you far greater profitability and extensive replay value.

- **Coin-op games come in many varieties.** Just about any game you can think of has a coin-op version available. Football, air hockey, video games, shooting games, skee-ball, basketball games, even video poker and blackjack machines that fit into your bar top: it's all available and it's all going to bring in a newer, younger customer for a minimum investment - or no investment at all.

Pinball Machines

The trusty pinball machine has been around since the late 1800s yet it still uses the same formula as the pinballs of old: lights, sound effects, the bounce of the ball, the "fwap" of the flipper and the lure of a high score. With a little smart thinking, your pinball machines can earn you a lot of money.

- **Install a pinball machine in your waiting area** - it makes a great distraction. If you keep the noise levels down so nearby customers don't get annoyed, they can be a great earner. Coin-op companies can bring you the latest pinball machines for free and will split all profits with you at the end of the month. And at $0.50 a game, a machine only needs to be played ten times a day to bring you $75 a month in profit sharing. That's not a bad return on zero investment.

- **Vintage machines**. Invest in a vintage pinball machine rather than getting a coin-op company to bring in a high-tech modern machine on which you'll have to split your profits. Older machines cost far less to buy and a lot less to maintain, and the appeal of an old machine will bring back a lot of memories for your older patrons. Machines such as these can be purchased through online auctions such as eBay (www.ebay.com).

- **Outright purchase.** If you choose to purchase your own pinball machines, look in the classified ads, or at local auctions for the best deal. Of course, purchasing your own machine will mean you're responsible for its maintenance, so look for a machine that either comes with an array of spare parts or has been fully serviced recently. The older the machine, the tougher it becomes to track down spare parts when the time comes to repair them.

Darts

Long a bar-game institution, the old dartboard has moved to high-tech of late. Gone are the old days of having patrons throw pointy darts around the room and hoping nobody puts out an eye; with high-tech alternatives, the only thing flying will be your profit margin.

- **New technology.** Look at what's available on the market today. The trusty old dartboard has received a technological boost. Coin-operated dart systems not only keep score for your patrons, but they also bring in a new source of revenue. Turnkey systems can be purchased or brought in under a profit-sharing deal. Though old hands at darts may frown at the changes, the new breed of player is very comfortable with new technology and is prepared to pay to use it.

- **Dedicated area.** Even if you can't be bothered with a coin-op version of darts, it still pays to set aside an area for a dartboard. Tournaments and leagues can bring in a steady flow of new customers - and they're almost always hard drinkers.

Pool Tables

Who doesn't enjoy going out for an evening of pool? In fact, many bars base their entire business on the lure of this age-old game. What's more, the money that can be brought in from the tables is perhaps the most lucrative of any coin-op game.

- **Investment.** If you're looking for a sound investment in coin-op machinery that won't cost you a lot to maintain, pool tables are the way to go. When they do need servicing, repairs are relatively simple. And there can be no doubting the pool table's appeal to the masses. Unlike computerized coin-ops, they don't need to be updated frequently. Having a pool table supplier bring in tables for free is a valid option if you want to simplify things, but you'll be giving up half of your profits for that convenience. Spend a little, make a lot.

- **Space.** One of the worst things that a pool player can experience is a lack of space. So make sure you give each table ample room in which to play properly. Nobody likes to have to leave his seat so that he doesn't get smacked in the head with a cue during a shot.

- **Maintain your pool equipment.** Bent cues, missing balls, no chalk on the end of the table; these are all small things that will drive a dedicated pool player elsewhere. Remember, a dedicated pool player will stay and drink and pump dollars into a table all night long.

- **Run a weekly pool tournament.** Offering up a $50 prize to the winner of a weekly pool tournament is bound to bring you many times that in beer sales from the contestants, their friends and those who just like to watch. Increase your prize and increase your tournament's appeal.

- **Make your tables free, for maximum customer draw.** Pool tables are a great source of income, but have you considered setting them to play for free for at least part of the week? It's an irrefutable fact that pool tables draw drinkers into your establishment, so if your venue is empty on a Monday, why not make that free pool night and fill the bar? You might as well fill the joint and make some money in drinks!

Jukeboxes

For years, hospitality venues have seen the appeal and profitability of the jukebox, and the modern day hasn't changed the jukebox's universal appeal. In fact, some venues not only make a fortune from their jukebox, they also serve as the venues' number-one draw.

- **Never bring a generic jukebox into your establishment.** The biggest jukebox suppliers will fill your machine with music your customers have heard before and are unlikely to pay to hear again, whereas purchasing your own jukebox and filling it with CDs that you know have local appeal is a far better option. It'll cost a little more initially, but if you get rid of the discs that don't pay and leave in the ones that do, you'll soon be earning a whole lot more - and not splitting profits.

- **Keep an eye on volume level.** Your bar staff should never let the jukebox get ridiculously loud, nor should they let it be so low that it can't be heard. Remember, some customers have terrible taste, and a loud jukebox inflicts that poor taste on everyone.

- **A video jukebox can be a great lure.** But a VideoCD jukebox is an even better draw for one simple reason; you can create your own VideoCDs and fashion them to suit. For example, filling a VideoCD jukebox with karaoke music that shows on your TV screens turns your venue into an impromptu sing-along bar whenever someone plays a great song. Not many bars use this technology yet, but the smart ones will jump all over it.

- **The tabletop jukebox.** It may be a relic of a bygone era, but having that much point-of-sale presence is certainly a great way to increase revenues. These units sit on the side of your seating booths and are constantly in your customers' faces, tempting them to drop in a few coins. This popularity can create a musical backlog of selections, but that certainly won't hurt your bottom line.

Beer Isn't The Only Beverage That Comes Brewed

Coffee-based beverages have long been a bar staple, but times have changed and nowadays people aren't content to have their coffee from any old drip-coffee machine.

- **Espresso.** Today's coffee drinkers want to know that the coffee they're buying is quality, and they want espresso or nothing. Over the last decade, coffee making has become more of an art form than ever, and if you're keeping up with consumer trends, you better have an espresso machine on the premises.

- **Baristas?** Employees that know their way around a coffee machine and a bar are known as baristas. And though a true barista is a whiz with the espresso machine and can command a far-higher salary, for the most part you won't need an expert at the helm of your espresso machine, just someone competent who can train others to a similar level of competence. Make the coffee machine part of your orientation for new staff; your patrons will love you for it.

- **Investment.** A good espresso machine doesn't come cheap, but the content of a good cup of coffee does. So while the initial investment in coffee-making hardware can be recouped in a matter of months, from that point on you're looking at a profit margin equal to, or even higher than, that of traditional alcohol sales. Make that investment now!

- **Promotions.** Promote your new coffee service, if need be, with giveaways and specials - even the occasional coffee on the house. Your regulars will surely appreciate the offer of a free cup at the end of a big night, and the detoxification that the caffeine promotes might even help them get home a little more safely.

- **Ambiance.** An integral part of today's coffee-drinking experience is where you sip it. Just throwing an espresso machine into a sports bar won't turn the place into a caffeine addict's paradise. Think outdoor seating, plants, shade-cloth, soft jazz, lamp heaters, a good wine menu... you get the idea.

Bars Need Cigars

We all know that smoking is on the downward slide, but few realize that cigar smoking is actually on the increase. More and more, affluent bar patrons and those merely seeking something different are turning to the humidor for a relaxing smoke. What this means to you is an opportunity to profit from supplying what your customers want. But while cigars sales are well and good as a profit alternative, also consider the many other aspects of this trend that can bring you a fine wedge of cash. Cigar smoking is far more than a habit; it's a ritual. And if you're selling cigars, you also need to supply the tools and atmosphere that go with the experience.

- **Start with a mood.** The cigar is all about relaxation, so replacing your standard bar-style tables and chairs with wooden coffee tables, leather chairs and/or sofas is a great start. Keeping the music low, making sure there's a good ventilation system and ensuring seclusion from the rest of your bar operation is the finishing touch. If you can fit out a room or a section of your venue in this fashion, you'll find cigar smokers - and others who just enjoy a quieter experience - making a beeline for your door.

- **Accessorize!** Giving your customers something to take home with your logo on it is a great way to remind them to come back. Anything from matchbooks to lighters to cigar cutters is a great (and inexpensive) option for your venue.

- **Don't open the door without a humidor.** Cigars are susceptible to outside conditions, which means savvy cigar bars provide a temperature-controlled humidor for their cigar products. These can be freestanding structures or built into the existing facilities. While a good humidor is protecting your cigars, it also serves as a great POS display for them.

- **If you can't cut a cigar, you can't smoke it.** And so it goes that a multitude of cigar cutters are available for resale. The price of a good cutter depends on the style, blade, quality and materials, but most range in price from as little as $2.50 to a thousand times that amount. Variety is key, and if you offer a good range of cutters for sale, some with your logo on them, you can bring in a great profit with a small investment.

- **Serving equipment.** This is another important part of the professional cigar bar. Presentation boxes that hold a number of cigars and can be brought to the table by a server are a very elegant way to go. Individual cigar cases can be an excellent add-on product for when you make a cigar sale.

- **Cigar matches.** Very different from standard tissue matches, they offer yet another source of revenue for your cigar bar. Cigar smokers traditionally don't like the flavor a common sulfur-based match gives their smoke, but cedar matches, which are slightly longer and far more odorless, are right up their alley. Cover any matchbooks you sell with your logo (every marketing opportunity is valuable) and sell them for a nominal fee - or give them away free with every cigar purchase.

- **Cigar lighters.** Far different from the everyday cigarette lighter, cigar lighters use butane. The reason for this variation is the same as the reasoning behind cedar matches: butane burns cleaner and imparts very little taste on the cigar itself. However, they are more expensive. Stock up and sell to your hearts content!

- **Ashtrays** - another important aspect of the cigar bar and while just about any standard ashtray can do the job, elongated ashtrays with deep cigar resting channels allow your smokers to put their smokes down without spilling them about. Cigar ashtrays come in many materials, from glass to ceramic, marble to metal. They top off the appeal of your cigar bar nicely.

LAYOUT OF A TYPICAL BAR

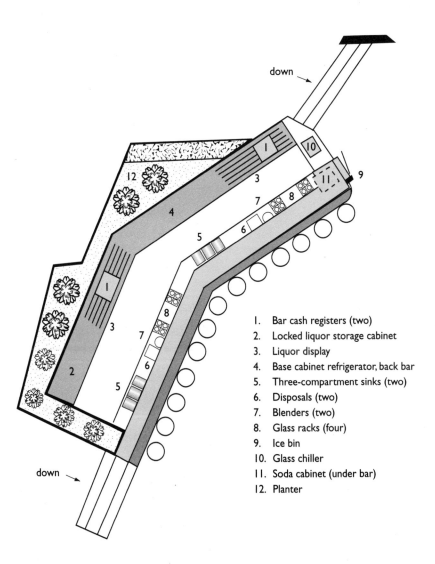

1. Bar cash registers (two)
2. Locked liquor storage cabinet
3. Liquor display
4. Base cabinet refrigerator, back bar
5. Three-compartment sinks (two)
6. Disposals (two)
7. Blenders (two)
8. Glass racks (four)
9. Ice bin
10. Glass chiller
11. Soda cabinet (under bar)
12. Planter

INDEX

Your #1 Source for Books, Videos, Training Materials, Tools, and Software

Especially for the Food Service, Restaurant and Hospitality Industry Professional!

Our Web site was designed with your convenience in mind. The search feature makes it easy to find exactly what you're looking for and there are over 1,000 items from which to choose. Orders may be placed by using our online 100% Secure Shopping Cart. Simply the best reference for the food service professional!

If you enjoyed this book, order the entire series!

The FOOD Service Professional
GUIDE TO SERIES

1-800-541-1336 Call toll-free
24 hours a day, 7 days a week.
Or fax completed form to:
1-352-622-5836. Order Online!
Just go to **www.atlantic-pub.com**
for fast, easy, secure ordering.

Qty	Order Code	Book Title	Price	Total
	Item # RMH-02	THE RESTAURANT MANAGER'S HANDBOOK	$79.95	
	Item # FS1-01	Restaurant Site Location	$19.95	
	Item # FS2-01	Buying & Selling A Restaurant Business	$19.95	
	Item # FS3-01	Restaurant Marketing & Advertising	$19.95	
	Item # FS4-01	Restaurant Promotion & Publicity	$19.95	
	Item # FS5-01	Controlling Operating Costs	$19.95	
	Item # FS6-01	Controlling Food Costs	$19.95	
	Item # FS7-01	Controlling Labor Costs	$19.95	
	Item # FS8-01	Controlling Liquor, Wine & Beverage Costs	$19.95	
	Item # FS9-01	Building Restaurant Profits	$19.95	
	Item # FS10-01	Waiter & Waitress Training	$19.95	
	Item # FS11-01	Bar & Beverage Operation	$19.95	
	Item # FS12-01	Successful Catering	$19.95	
	Item # FS13-01	Food Service Menus	$19.95	
	Item # FS14-01	Restaurant Design	$19.95	
	Item # FS15-01	Increasing Restaurant Sales	$19.95	
	Item # FSALL-01	**Entire 15-Book Series**	**$199.95**	

Best Deal! SAVE 33%
All 15 books for $199.95

Subtotal	
Shipping & Handling	
Florida 6% Sales Tax	
TOTAL	

SHIP TO:

Name_____Phone(_____)_____

Company Name_____

Mailing Address _____

City _____State _____Zip _____

FAX _____E-mail _____

❏ My check or money order is enclosed   ❏ Please send my order COD   ❏ My authorized purchase order is attached

❏ Please charge my: ❏ Mastercard ❏ VISA ❏ American Express ❏ Discover

Card # ☐☐☐☐ – ☐☐☐☐ – ☐☐☐☐ – ☐☐☐☐   Expires ☐☐☐☐

Please make checks payable to: **Atlantic Publishing Company** • 1210 SW 23 Place • Ocala, FL 34474-7014
USPS Shipping/handling: add $5.00 first item, $2.50 each additional or $15.00 for the whole set. Florida residents
PLEASE add the appropriate sales tax for your county.